M000204985

© 2019 by Benedicte Maurseth
translation © 2019 by Bruce Thomson

ISBN: 978-1-949597-05-9
Library of Congress Control Number: 2019934558

Originally published as *Å vera ingenting. Samtalar med spelemannen Knut Hamre.*
© 2014 by Det Norske Samlaget, Oslo.
Published by agreement with Hagen Agency AS.

This translation has been published with the financial support of NORLA,
Norwegian Literature Abroad.

published by:

Terra Nova Press
NEWARK   CALLICOON   MATSALU

Publisher: David Rothenberg
Editor-in-Chief: Evan Eisenberg
Translator: Bruce Thomson
Editor: Tyran Grillo
Designer: Martin Pedanik
Cover Photo: Knut Bry

set in Spectral and Gotham

printed by Tallinn Book Printers, Tallinn Estonia
on Munken Kristall paper, flexibound

1 2 3 4 5 6 7 8 9 10

www.terranovapress.com

Distributed by the MIT Press, Cambridge, Massachusetts and London, England

To Be Nothing

For my master, in humble gratitude

CONTENTS

PRELUDE

I began my schooling in the Hardanger fiddle as a little girl, when my master Knut Hamre (b. 1952) came to my local music school in Eidfjord to give me lessons. Back then, I didn't know he was, and still is, considered one of Norway's most prominent Hardanger fiddlers of all time. I also had no concept of the depth and richness of the centuries-old folk music tradition I was entering into, even though it came from my own home region of Hardanger, in Western Norway. Nor did I know what a profound anchorage and identity I would develop as a human being through this fiddle music—*slåttemusikk* in Norwegian— and its history. Being just a child, I was looking for something to feed my spirit. Yet somehow, perhaps by sheer coincidence, folk music became my primary form of artistic expression.

My master has always been a wise man and good listener. He taught me about my local folk music tradition through a wide lens. I learned its craft, its history, and its techniques, and with them a vast repertoire of fiddle tunes, shared and played by hundreds of fiddlers from the 1600s to the present day. He taught me his theories and philosophy of life, which he so succinctly and mysteriously calls the "to be nothing" approach—a state of being in service to an art, to a tradition, and to your students. I learned, too, about the healing and therapeutic qualities of music.

Playing was naturally the centerpiece of our sessions, and Knut taught all of this music through an age-old tradition, whereby I copied what I could see and hear in lieu of formal notation. But I learned the most from our discussions together, covering topics inclusive of and far beyond music. We even discussed other forms of artistic expression, religion, literature, philosophy, and pedagogy, among other practical concerns. It was just as much an education in life as in the fiddle music tradition of Hardanger. I have been learning from Knut for almost thirty years. Extracts from our discussions have been gathered into this book.

But what is this Hardanger fiddle of which I speak? And what is this tradition I was becoming a part of? For any newcomers to Norwegian folk music, the Hardanger fiddle is considered to be the national instrument of Norway. The name "Hardanger fiddle" (*hardingfele*) comes from the Hardangerfjord, where the instrument made its first appearance in the 1600s, the pride of some exceptionally talented luthiers. Gradually the instrument spread to other parts of the world, but is most prominent in the southern half of its narrow homeland.

The Hardanger fiddle is an instrument that, in terms of construction, bears clear resemblances to the violin. Yet it stands out in that it also has a number of understrings, or sympathetic strings, as one would find on the viola d'amore, Swedish nyckelharpa, and a number of other similar instruments. The number of understrings on Hardanger fiddles has changed over time, but today they typically have either four or five. When the bow is drawn across one or more of the four playing strings, the understrings sing out in harmony, thus providing the fiddle with its distinctive sound. The bridge itself is less arched than that of the violin, which makes the Hardanger fiddle more suitable for the *bordunspel* (double stopping) common in the region's music.

The rhythm and structure of this fiddle's music may sound odd to listeners of contemporary Western music. Melodies are formed of short musical segments that twirl around each other repeatedly, each time with tiny variations. These motifs join to form musical phrases that then weave together in their own logical way. It is not through counting beats but by listening to the melody that a fiddler knows when to move on to the next segment. This means that, unlike more mainstream genres,

Hardanger fiddle music does not fit easily into more familiar musical structures, such as the AABA format you hear in pop music, old-time dancing, and standard repertoires. Neither is *slåttemusikk* based around the chords of a piano, but is instead modal.

The Hardanger fiddle repertoire is complex and demanding. Like Norwegian accents, each fiddle tradition around the country differs greatly in tonality and rhythm. Traditionally the Hardanger fiddle has been performed solo, and has been immensely important in dance. Yet over the last hundred years, one sees the Hardanger fiddle being paired more and more often with other instruments and genres. *Slåttemusikk* used to be the day-to-day music of Norway's villages and valleys, and fiddlers were always present and playing at rituals or ceremonies such as weddings, wakes, parties, or public holidays.

For a long while, fiddlers were seen by some as almost-holy men, although their status has varied greatly over the years, particularly in the differing attitudes of town and country folk, but also more generally through the 1800s as new dances such as waltzes, polkas, and the schottische began supplanting Norway's older forms of fiddle music. During this period, instruments such as the piano and diatonic button accordion also became more popular, and in several locations began competing with the fiddle. Many Hardanger fiddlers probably felt like they were losing their well-established positions, as age-old fiddle pieces were threatened with extinction. The 1800s also saw the development of more extreme forms of Christianity. The Hardanger fiddle was seen by many during this time as the "devil's instrument." Many Hardanger fiddlers stopped playing altogether, going so far as to sell or burn their fiddles for fear of social banishment, if not eternal damnation in the afterlife.

The 19th century was a complex time for Norway. After four centuries of Danish rule we finally received our own constitution in 1814, only to be governed by a Swedish king after Denmark-Norway lost to Sweden in the Napoleonic wars. Still, many Norwegians yearned for total independence and began nation-building. Norwegian fiddle players and their oldest forms of music were promoted and politically exploited by romantic nationalists to establish a sense of national identity. It was also during this time that fiddlers went from playing at dances and weddings to hosting more traditional concerts on open stages. Many of these fiddlers achieved widespread success and staggering wealth, especially once they started going on concert tours in America.

Toward the end of the 19th century, various Norwegian associations began arranging competitions, which we now refer to as *kappleik*, to improve the prominence of solo fiddling. At first, *kappleik* were restricted to solo players of the Hardanger fiddle and the normal fiddle (called *flatfele* or *fele* among traditional players, and fitted with a flatter bridge then the modern violin). Only the older forms of fiddling tunes, such as *gangar*, *springar*, *halling*, and *huldreslått* were performed, and not old-time dance music. Today, *kappleikar* also allow competitions in traditional singing called *kveding*, as well as the jaw harp, solo and traditional paired dancing, the willow flute, the *langeleik* (a Norwegian dulcimer), and much more. The modern-day national *kappleik* is one of the largest annual folk music events in Norway, drawing crowds of thousands.

After the Second World War and into the 1950s and 1960s, folk music fell quiet in many Norwegian villages as Anglo-American culture and music gradually took over. Anything "too Norwegian" began to wane in popularity. But a few young people, including my master, Knut Hamre, managed to salvage the Hardanger tradition. The Hardanger fiddle has also been dominated by men throughout its history, which means that my playing it as a woman is a relatively new phenomenon. Having said that, contemporary research into female fiddlers shows that in certain places in Norway, women were successful fiddlers at weddings and dances in the 18th and early 19th centuries, but that this tradition eventually came to an end or at least fell by the wayside for quite some time. From the 1960s onward, there have been at least as many women as men playing the Hardanger or normal fiddle.

To Be Nothing is a book about art and pedagogy through the eyes and ears of a fiddle player. I decided to write it after realizing the open-ended and universal nature of my master's thoughts and knowledge, and how they could be transferred to other cultures and communities. This is how the book has been received in Norway. Artists, teachers, psychologists, consultants, priests, and more have used it to help them in their own fields. I hope my mentor's thoughts and knowledge can contribute just as much as they travel out into the wider world.

Benedicte Maurseth, April 2019

Do the Next Man a Favor

He came down from
the mountains, heading home,
got himself ferried from Osa
out to Øydvinsto.
He was open-handed
and offered to pay.

But the man from Osa
would have none of it.
I want to pay
—I can't reach you
to return the favor.
Then do the next man
a favor,
said the man from Osa
and shoved off.

Olav H. Hauge, 1956
(Translated by Olav Grinde)

FOREWORD

I was born in 1959, Knut Hamre in 1952. I grew up in the parish of Strandebarm, Knut in Granvin. Our age gap isn't particularly large, and neither is the distance between the villages of Strandebarm and Granvin, or our respective homes of Fosse and Folkedal within them. At least not in kilometers. There was, however, a deep cultural divide between the two areas. Hardanger fiddle music was alive and well in Granvin where Knut grew up, whereas the Strandebarm of my childhood had none at all. Or if it did, it only ever took place behind closed doors.

My fascination with music started at an early age, and I took to the music I knew, which wasn't Hardanger fiddle music but Anglo-American rock. From around the age of twelve, I would waste away countless hours with my guitar, just as Knut was spending hours and hours of his adolescence playing the Hardanger fiddle. We must even have been around the same age when we first played at a dance. While I was in a band, blasting rock and other popular music, he was playing the Hardanger fiddle and becoming part of a noble, longstanding, local tradition.

At around that time, my head teacher in Strandebarm heard me play guitar and decided that I showed talent. He thought I needed to start playing the violin, raised the issue with my parents, and one day a man—who I presumed was somehow connected with Kvam parish's municipal arts council—arrived at our house with a violin, a pitch pipe, and a textbook on playing the violin. There was no talk of tuition. He simply told me to start playing. I never managed to teach myself how to even tune the violin.

When my sixteen-year-old self gave up on music and turned to writing, the world didn't miss out on much. In all honesty, I wish I had spent all that time and motivation on tunes from

Hardanger instead of imitating American songs and lyrics. (My bandmates and I used to listen to records, then scribble down the lyrics and teach ourselves to play the songs as best we could. Our English was a bit odd, I can promise you.)

Why did life turn out this way? For several years, my grandfather Olav K. Fosse (1896-1969), who lived in the house closest to our childhood home, found employment as a master of ceremonies at weddings—*kjøkemeister* in Norwegian. This was at a time when a Hardanger wedding ceremony could last for three full days, and this old position of toastmaster would lead the celebrations by singing solo acapella songs for different parts of the wedding. He would often attend these ceremonies with his neighbor, a fiddler named Peder Haukås (1898-1974). I remember Peder from when I was little. Yet no one breathed a word to me about his playing the Hardanger fiddle. I do, however, have a prominent memory of my father telling me about another fiddler, this one from Valdres, who my grandfather used to bring along to weddings, and whose name was Anders Bonde, known simply as "Bonden" (1850-1936). When my father was young, Bonden lived in the first house he would come to walking down the road. It was a small wooden crofter's cottage nestled against the fjord, almost beneath the shoreline. My father, Kristoffer Fosse (b. 1929), says that back then Bonden was *the* great fiddler, and recounts one occasion when he was little, listening from his grandfather's lap as Bonden played "soft and clear." And yet, by the time I was growing up, all that was gone. Had the Hardanger fiddle and her music been forgotten or hidden away? What happened?

Several years would pass before the treasures of Hardanger fiddle music were revealed to me, when I happened to perform a reading with Håkon Høgemo. Yet in that moment, this instrument and its unique melodies were at last brought so close to me that I couldn't help but hear them. Had this music, this instrument, truly existed for centuries in my own hometown, without me having the faintest idea? If so, how? What went wrong?

Later, before I gave up performing readings, I developed a preference for doing so alongside players of the Hardanger fiddle. I gave readings not only with Håkon Høgemo, but also Knut Hamre and Benedicte Maurseth. These three were my guides into the Hardanger fiddle world. Håkon, Knut, and Benedicte have not only unveiled a whole new world of music to me, but also given me countless insights into both life and art. I am always struck by how different art forms, be they musical or literary, can have so much in common. Everything of importance is universal. Through the conversations between Knut Hamre and his mentee of countless years, the prominent Hardanger fiddle player Benedicte Maurseth, *To Be Nothing* intricately explores these universals so that other people might also share their wisdom. Yet we also learn how an ancient musical culture might be salvaged in a modern era when the age-old custom of passing down knowledge from fiddler to fiddler via one-on-one tutoring is being steadily institutionalized by education in state-owned musical schools for children and other higher educational institutions. The Norwegian folk music tradition is undergoing monumental changes. If my own upbringing is anything to judge by, then something desperately needed to be done. *To Be Nothing* is the best kind of proof that something was.

Jon Fosse

A FIDDLE POET'S
UPBRINGING

1962 | In his home village of Folkedal, Granvin parish, Knut
Hamre is knocking on a neighbor's door. He is ten years old and
holds his fiddle case in one hand. He hasn't been invited. Yet he
keeps knocking on every single door he comes across in this tiny
hamlet, with its houses, smallholdings, and smokeries, winding
his way up and into the mountains toward Voss. He has to play
his fiddle. *Has* to. For himself and for others. Why should he
care whether his visits are appropriate? He only thinks about
playing. Fiddling is like breathing, and for Knut, it is the only
thing that has meaning. The music can raise his spirits, along
with the spirits of anyone else who needs it. Knut has no idea
where this hunger comes from. He plays all day, every day:
before school, at breaktime, and after he goes home. He forgets
to eat and sleep and turns up at school wearing Wellington
boots and an oversized raincoat, while his fellow pupils still run
around barefoot in the sunshine.

The neighbor opens his door and sees it's that little boy,
Knut. Again. Yet Knut is invited in and plays for them right
there in their living room, tune upon tune. Melodies learned
from the radio, his parents (Marta and Knut J. Hamre), or any
of the other houses nearby that happen to have a fiddle lying
around, regardless of how much they play. This is how it is in
the Folkedal of Knut's childhood, as in the other hamlets of
Granvin, such as Kvanndal and Eide. Everyone plays the fiddle.
Knut plays his heart out and in return he receives a glass of red
currant juice and a hearty thank you from the neighbor's wife.
They send him and his fiddle off home again, only this time
carrying their gramophone player under one arm, along with
their records of Knut's heroes: Halldor Meland, Ola Mosafinn,
and Eiliv Smedal. If they hadn't handed them over, he would
probably have remained sitting there, playing for the rest of the
day. Knut goes home and is in heaven.

Knut Hamre's life will eventually come to revolve around two main purposes: to play his fiddle, and to teach music to the next generation. In both respects, he is outstanding. Knut is the poet fiddler, at once deeply intimate and deeply absent. A master and a "nothing." Gentle. Wise. Selfless. A trendsetter who forms new melodies out of the old tunes singing from the land around him.

THE LITTLE CROSS

1990 | Late spring in Maurseth, Eidfjord parish. Eight-year-old me strolls into the kitchen of the family hotel. I watch from the window as the school bus turns around and trundles back down to the fjord. People in white catering uniforms dart around the kitchen as several hundred grams of well-done ground reindeer meat are poured into an enormous bowl. Everything in the hotel kitchen is big, from the pots, pans, and spatulas to the great vats of lingonberry.

In my hand is a white piece of paper from my music school: If I want to play an instrument, I'm allowed to choose one to start learning this August. My mum takes a break from reindeer frying to take a closer look at the form: guitar, piano, brass, Hardanger fiddle, organ, and more. So many to choose from.

"Maybe you should try the Hardanger fiddle?" my mum suggests. "After all, it comes from right here in Hardanger." I'm not sure I even know what a Hardanger fiddle is. But I make a clean checkmark next to *Hardanger fiddle* and stuff the note back into my schoolbag. Then I rush out on my bike, because a thaw has finally wiped the snow from our high-mountain roads.

The following autumn, I begin my musical education with my new mentor, Knut Hamre, a mentorship that will last for nearly thirty years, and still goes on today.

HORD,
HARD, ANGER,
ANGRE, ANGR, HARDANGER

"Never have the tones of fiddlesong made such impressions on me as those of the Hardanger fiddlers."

Ola Mosafinn

2012 | Dozens of red warning signs rise up to greet me as I shuffle along the road into Hardanger. They leer at me, reminding me that it would be wise to change gear. Steep slopes and sharp turns lie ahead. No matter the season, loose rocks, snow, or ice could come tumbling down the mountain at any moment and take you out. It makes no difference whether you approach the area from the north, south, east, or west. All those who enter the Hardangerfjord are gambling with their lives. In the early hours of this July morning, I'm driving from Bergen to Hardanger, destination: Granvin. There, I will meet my mentor, Knut Hamre. Despite having ceased to take lessons with him many years ago, we still meet regularly to play together. Sometimes I learn new tunes, sometimes I refresh the old ones. Most of our playing sessions are simply conversations about our music's tone and color. About personal expression, being in the moment, and musicians' stage fright. About music as healing or the dangers of conforming to ego. These conversations will likely go on for a very long time.

I always learn much from these conversations with my teacher. Sometimes we get stuck on the same issue, year after year. I remember Knut once telling me: "Master-student relationships don't really have exams and graduations." That's not how they are. If a mentorship works well, it can last a lifetime. But today we aren't going to play together like we normally do. Instead, we will visit all the local spots where Granvin's great fiddlers have lived over the years. I've wanted to do this for a long time: to tread in their footsteps, stand in their farms, and see the same scenery they saw. In folk music terms, Granvin is a Mecca. Here the knowledge of Hardanger fiddle music has survived in an unbroken succession of masters and students from 1600 right up to the present day. Neither is Granvin the only parish of its kind in Hardanger. Ullensvang parish also has a centuries-old tradition of handing down music from master to student. Such traditions, in fact, are actually found everywhere Norwegian fiddlers have lived.

Still, Granvin stands out in certain regards: due in part to the unbroken line of students and teachers, but also its wealth of outstanding musical pieces and fiddlers. Today I will see with my own eyes what I have been told ever since I was a little girl, and what has become something of a fairy tale for me: that in the Granvin of the 1960s, little Knut Hamre could have popped into just about any house he fancied if he wanted to learn a new tune, because back then fiddle players could be found in more or less a quarter of the parish's farms. (I remember Knut once telling me that locals would sometimes raffle off fiddles instead of cakes during village festivals.) As I drive down the Toka Gorge into Norheimsund, I reflect to myself how it wasn't at all like that when I was little. Folk music wasn't something that interested people in my family, or back home in Eidfjord, with a few exceptions. Actually, I reckon it's rather mind-boggling that I still even play the Hardanger fiddle. I don't come from some kind of folk-savvy family, where everyone plays and competes at *kappleikar*, and I certainly didn't have any folk music communities nearby to support me. For a long time, despite Knut's gentle encouragements, I was determined not to play at any of my music school's Christmas or summer assemblies, or attend any *kappleikar*, courses, or group rehearsals. Whether because of my shy, introverted personality, or because I grew up in a place far-flung from everything and with little public transport, I had still hardly done any of this by the time I passed my driving test.

For a long while I don't think I really knew who my teacher was, despite what people kept telling me: "You must know how immensely lucky you are to be taught by Knut Hamre himself!" On the few occasions when, as a teenager, I attended folk music gatherings, I was astonished that people kept whispering and staring at Knut whenever he walked by, and that the whole congregation would fall silent the moment he picked up his fiddle to play a little tune. For me, he was always just "Knut." So why did I keep playing over all those years? I don't quite understand it myself.

In truth, my journey from ticking that fateful box marked *Hardanger fiddle* to fulltime Hardanger fiddler feels like one big stroke of luck. The explanation behind it is a mixture of Knut's infectious, boundless love for playing, the incredible music itself, and how blissfully alone I felt with the fiddle. Through this timeless music, I entered a timeless place. I felt so fortunate that once a week I was allowed to spend time in a run-down classroom just listening to fiddle music while other lessons were going on at the school. In a heartbeat I could disappear into something different and beautiful, yet somehow recognizable. Only then did I realize how intuitively I was craving something so deep.

Knut would occasionally come out with strange, outlandish statements during our sessions. Phrases like "I am a nothing" or "the fiddle is an extension of the heart and the bow an extension of the hand." Yet because Knut never gave one answer but several of them, I never stopped asking questions. Knut was a paradox. I often left our sessions feeling like a big, walking question mark. Yet I always felt better and more sure of myself than when I walked in. It's still like that to this day.

Knut has always entertained my quirks. When I was little, I only ever wanted to learn all the weird and wonderful scordatura (fiddle tunings) we have in Hardanger, and stretch any dance tunes into *lydarslåttar* (tunes played for listening and not dancing) so their notes had time to breathe and sing. I still do. I've always been hopeless when it comes to any sort of group playing or typical dance tunes, because I would much rather take the time to bring color to each tone and write short poems with my fiddle. In Zen Buddhism, there is a teaching that states, "A master who cannot bow to their student cannot bow to Buddha," and Knut has spoken about musical freedom and equal worth between masters and students for as long as I can remember. But masters aren't always this way. As part of such a long musical heritage, each teacher must strike the perfect balance between their own art and their duty of preserving knowledge. I know, for example, that Knut had it much harder than me. When he was younger, he had a great deal of pressure placed on him to preserve the Hardanger tradition, since he was one of the few young talents—if not the *only* young talent—on the fiddle at the time. For this reason, in the 1960s and 70s, Knut was seen by many as the "sole heir" to Hardanger's folk music.

As for the true reason why I became so completely hooked on the Hardanger fiddle by the end of my teens, I can't quite put it into words. I just played. It felt natural and necessary. But perhaps it also stems from the fact that one never quite reaches the end of this music. Just as Knut always gave more than one answer, so too does Hardanger fiddle music. It is a beautiful, complex, and almost magical sound that provides you with something to love and cherish your entire life.

Further along the Toka Gorge, the road steepens. As I brake and shift into second gear and crawl down the slopes, the gray mist over the gorge resolves into a vast and verdant landscape.

I have read up on the name Hardanger. It is a combination of *Hard*, from *Hordernes*, meaning "belonging to the Horder people" of the region, and the old Norse and Norwegian words *angr, angre*, or *anger*. These refer to a narrow, tightly wedged area at the bottom of a fjord. I arrive in Norheimsund and realize how much the name makes sense. As I roll these Old Norwegian words around my mouth, I can't stop myself from thinking about Geirr Tveitt, a composer who lived here and the man behind the orchestral work *A Hundred Folk Tunes from Hardanger*, Op. 151. Tveitt adored the region's folk music, especially its use of microtones[1] and modes.[2]

On far-off peaks I can make out Hardanger's infamous electricity pylons, the red-and-white "monster masts." Next to catch my eye is the Christian meeting house. I have often said, with a hint of irony, that in Hardanger wherever there are meeting houses you won't find fiddlers, cider, or apple trees. It's not entirely correct, of course, and as if to prove me wrong, the next things I see are rows of well-kept apple trees. But there haven't been nearly as many fiddlers here as in the villages further up the Hardangerfjord.

White caravans with German number plates fly past me as I look at the white makeshift church and ponder how the roles and social statuses of fiddlers have changed over the years. They started out almost as holy men, needed as they were to carry out weddings and funerals. They have inspired awe and mystery for as long as the Hardanger fiddle has existed. They went on to become a visible sign of religious belief and conduct in the mid-1800s, when the Lutheran Pietism of the Hans Nilsen Hauge (1771-1824) movement compelled much of the Norwegian peasantry to confront their moral guilt. Many fiddle players threw their bows and fiddles into bonfires and used their hands for prayer instead. All this changed, however, when the

Norwegian cultural elite—master violinist Ole Bull (1810-1880), for example, and other artists—decided that peasant culture, with the fiddler known as "Myllarguten" (Torgeir Augundsson, 1801-1872)[3] as its important political symbol, should be promoted to help the Norwegian public's self-esteem toward a dissolution of union with Sweden. At this point, many began referring to *slåttemusikk* as "national music" and the region's traditional rural clothing as Norway's "national costume." Yet the Hardanger fiddlers of the era were letting the oldest forms of their music (such as *rull*, *gangar*, *springar*, *lydarslåttar*, *huldreslåttar*, and *brureslåttar*) be replaced by contemporary, international styles of folk dance, such as waltzes, marches, the schottische, and the Hamborgar (a type of polka in 2/4). This was because at the time these styles, known collectively as *gamaldans* or "old-time dances," were all the rage. In hopes of refreshing the status of *slåttemusikk* in Norway, in 1896 the language organization Vestmannalaget established the first nationwide *kappleik* in Bergen. As each fiddler finished playing their tunes, the famous composer Edvard Grieg (1843-1907) sat applauding from the front bench.

In the 1930s and 40s, many Norwegians felt that national spirit was getting out of hand, which may have been one of the reasons why folk music stagnated to the extent it did during the 1950s and 60s. Fiddlers and folk music essentially fell off the charts in these years, while The Beatles and other Anglo-American music was heard blasting from record players. But then in the 1970s, and likely influenced by Norway's "No" vote to the European Communities (EC) membership referendum of 1972, the "green wave" arrived. With it came a belief that agriculture and folk music, along with the written standard (Nynorsk) and dialects of rural Norway, should be respected and cultivated. Norwegian folk music has been on the rise ever since the 1970s, thanks to increasing numbers of fiddle players and venues willing to promote the music. It has become an accepted genre of the same caliber as jazz, rock, and classical music. Despite this inclusion, folk music today is almost an underground genre compared to the years leading up to the 1950s, when it was still a practical part of daily life in most villages. The only aspect that sets modern folk music apart from before is all the women fiddle players now taking part in the art form.

THE WESTERNERS

The white meeting houses gradually disappear into my rear view mirror as I drive toward Øystese. I pop in a CD of *slåttar* from Hardanger. In Norwegian, *slått* (tune) is the lay term for a piece of folk music, whereas terms like *gangar* and *springar* refer to specific styles. The word *slått* originally comes from the verb *å slå* (to hit), as *slåttemusikk* was likely once played by "hitting" the strings on an instrument with a plectrum or fingers, back before the bow came into use.

I've heard many people describe Hardanger fiddle music as an exclusive, inaccessible art form. When you take into account how each piece, with its strange rhythms, tones, and recurring melodies, has a radically different form and structure to the more regular rhythms of today's music, it is no wonder people feel this way. *Slåttemusikk* demands a lot from its listeners. The genre has its own rules, just as Indian ragas and the blues have theirs.

I offer an imaginary wave as I pass a house in Vallandshovden, where master fiddler Halldor Meland (1884-1972) lived out his final years. Meland was actually from Ullensvang parish, and was a great musician. He was one of the very few fiddle players prior to the Second World War who was able to make a living solely by performing. He traveled throughout Norway, Denmark, and Sweden giving concerts, and even had his own impresario. The proud, crass Meland turned much of Hardanger's repertoire upside down, spawning great debate and a new style of playing. He was second to none. I suddenly remember Knut once telling me about the time he met Meland, together with fiddlers Anders Kjerland and Jens Amundsen. Knut was fourteen years old, and had just played for his musical idol as well as he possibly could. Meland was silent. He raised his aged bowing hand and gave Knut a few slow pats on the head. Only later did Knut hear from fellow villagers what Meland had said afterward: "I hope the Hardangers take care of that boy."

You can find everything in the Hardanger repertoire, from short, straightforward pieces to rich, complex melodies. As I wind my way along the fjord's shores, I hum a tune composed by Meland called *Vestlendingen*, or "The Westerner." This *slått* has a strong character. Proud. Wise. And wrapped in a lyrical veil. Was this how Meland saw the Western Norwegians? Music from Hardanger is indeed often described as lyrical. Why are we able to find common features in these musical styles, despite their vast geographical spread? How have so many generations of fiddle players arrived at this shared poetry? What makes me hear this familiar resonance, which reminds me of meeting up with an old relative, in a tune that was thought up hundreds of years ago? Why do we keep coming back to this common sound? Is there some aesthetic that all Western Norwegians share? In any case, they must have been pretty stubborn, I think to myself as I lean into the steering wheel and glimpse a farmstead, sitting all alone on its slope. From a distance, the farm looks tiny, clinging desperately to the steep mountain in search of sun. What hard work it must have been. It's like watching a dandelion squeeze through a crack in asphalt. Evidence of human life and settlement in Hardanger dates all the way back to the Neolithic period, and many of the farms here are from the middle ages—all this despite a lack of fertile soil to go round. This must be why so many people from Hardanger have emigrated, or had to take up other professions alongside their farming, such as shipping, logging, fishing, trade, and the craft industry.

I pause at a red light and must wait before I cross the one-way Fyksesund Bridge. I gaze out over the fjord. It has always been the main artery of Hardanger. Every lake, river, and waterfall, to say little of the endless rain, will eventually gush out into the Hardangerfjord, adding to its ceaseless flow. A flow of people, a flow of ideas. I look out to the northeast, toward the side fjord that runs all the way out to the village of Botnen, deep in the middle of Fyksesund. Before the roads took over, Botnen used to be a vibrant village community. The fjord was its highway. First the world came by sail, then by steam, in addition to all the little wooden boats used in the region for general transport. The fjord also brought to Hardanger instrument-building knowhow. I wouldn't be surprised to learn that Bergen played an essential role in this. Bergen was Norway's largest city right up until the 1830s, and had been its foremost center of trade ever since the Hanseatic League established itself there in the 1350s. Bergen had a monopoly on Hardanger's trade for a long time.

The oldest Hardanger fiddle we know of is the famous "Jaastad fiddle," signed and dated in 1651 by Ole Jonsen Jaastad (1621-1694) from Ullensvang. Yet there is no doubt that, prior to Telemark's takeover in the 1800s, the craftsmen who had the deepest impact on the Hardanger fiddle's development were Isak Nielsen Skaar (1669-1759) and his son, Trond Isaksen Flatebø (1713-1772). Both lived in Botnen, just a short boat ride from where I'm waiting in my car. Their instruments are exceptional in terms of craftsmanship and sound, and are some of the best Hardanger fiddles I have played in my life. The complete works of Isak and Trond are vast and varied. People say Trond was one of the richest men in all of Western Norway when he passed away. Today we know that Isak and Trond, as well as the Bergen fiddle makers, made violins as well as Hardanger fiddles. The oldest surviving example of a made-in-Norway violin was created by Trond Isaksen Flatebø and dated 1764. This violin appeared out of nowhere in Copenhagen a few years ago, and my train of thought is suddenly cut off by a loud beeping behind me. A long line of cars has accumulated in the short while I sat there waiting for a green light.

Map of Granvin Municipality.

GRANVIN

I cross the fjord and ponder the fact that much of Hardanger's fiddle music is older than the fiddle itself. The earliest Hardanger fiddle player for whom we have concrete sources is Askjell Brattespe (1722-1807) from Ullensvang. Yet there isn't much reason to doubt that there were fiddlers beforehand who played something other than the Hardanger fiddle. Recent studies suggest that a variety of fiddles existed in the Hardanger region before the "Jaastad fiddle." There is a small fiddle case in the Voss Folkemuseum, for example, which is dated 1512. We also know from Old Norse literature that people in Bergen and many other parts of Norway played the fidel and the rebec in the Middle Ages, possibly up until the 1500s. In the records of crimes committed in Ullensvang between 1625-26 we find the following example: "Kristi Suermingsdatter ist slayn by mann af name Jens Spillemand [Jens the Fiddleplayer] and he hath fled." And from Kinsarvik in 1631: "Gunille N. wert slayn by vagrant and scoundrel, af name Spillers [Fiddlers], and he hath fled."

The fiddlers cut and ran whenever they caused too much trouble, I joke to myself as I finally lay eyes on Granvin's coat of arms. It shows a Hardanger fiddle, of course. In light of the area's musical heritage, this was an obvious choice. Granvin is right at the end of the Granvinsfjorden, its own little waterway in the north-eastern section of the Hardangerfjord. The parish looks pretty much like any other small village in Norway, with its solitary church, handful of houses, smattering of farms, a tired old gas station, and a community center. Most drivers in the Granvin area would probably go right past it, unless they happened to be hunting for fiddle music. Here, each road winds its way up to what used to be the great crossroads of Hardanger. So much impressive cultural history lies hidden up the village's every hill and down its every dale.

For centuries, Granvin has lived off its forest. Hardanger's oldest and most crucial lumber mill was in use here as early as 1653. By the 1800s, when steam had finally replaced sail, the center of Granvin, Eide, had developed into an industrial center with routes to Bergen, Haugesund, and Stavanger. The main road between Voss and Hardanger passed through Granvin. By the late 19th century it saw a great deal of tourist traffic, and Granvin even had a direct line from Newcastle in north-eastern England. But the First World War made it all grind to a halt.

Knut Hamre has lived in Granvin nearly his whole life. Today we are going to visit everywhere in the parish Hardanger fiddle players have lived. Right before I turn into the ferry port in Kvanndal, I imagine myself waving up at the Håstabø farm, where the fiddle player Olav Håstabø (1826-1899) lived for a time. An ancient oak stands next to the old lane, acting as a natural waymark for the turn leading up to the farm. I have been there several times in the past, both with Knut and on my own, just to spend a little time with Olav Håstabø, somehow. Håstabø was a poet on the Hardanger fiddle who arranged and composed a large amount of original pieces. All of them were rich in detail, emotive and lyrical. He was one of the most respected Hardanger fiddles of his time, but also subsisted as a tailor between his playing activities. Håstabø's obituary reads:

"When Olav had a thought he wanted off his chest, he let his fiddle draw it out. Then he would play *rull* and *springar* (the very best of the fjord's fiddle tunes) so true and fine, with such pure melody, and surrounded with such power and gentleness that it became scarred into my memory."

We don't know who wrote this obituary, and his gravestone no longer exists, but he was buried next to another great fiddler from the village, Lars Røynstrand (1822-1899), also known as "Halte-Lars" (Limping Lars). In Kvanndal, I roll up the drive of a small red house. Knut and his wife, Aud, have lived here for several years, ever since their eldest daughter took over their old farmstead in Folkedal, just five minutes' drive from Kvanndal. Olav Håstabø also lived in this red house for a time, as well as his nephew, Sjur Håstabø (1872-1945), also a fiddle player and known as "Nolten" (The Nock) after the hill his house was built on. Other great musicians have been through these doors as well, including the Voss fiddlers Nils Rekve and Ola Mosafinn, as well as the Telemark fiddlers Olav Bergland and Halvor, Hans, and Ola Flatland. It only makes sense that Knut now lives here, too. As I switch off the engine, my ears are met with the sounds of fiddle. Knut is playing away as usual. From where does he get all this drive and energy? Unlike so many musicians, including myself, not once have I ever heard him say he was tired of playing. I have bumped into him every now and then when he's out on an errand, and he always has his fiddle with him. Once or twice I raised the question of why he lugged his fiddle around when there wasn't any time to play. I could see from his face that he didn't really understand the question.

Eventually Knut wanders over to my car. His jacket is buttoned together in all the wrong places. Typical Knut. He couldn't care less about appearances, so he probably put it on in a hurry. What's more, even though he is quite a big, lofty man, his steps are light and careful. I've noticed this when we hike together, too. He positively floats along the path. Knut climbs quickly into the car, without saying so much as hello, and shoves a CD into the stereo right away. "Before we can do anything else, we have to listen to 'Håvards sorg' as played by Johannes Dale," he declares. So we sit and listen. When the recording ends, he is teary-eyed and exclaims, "Isn't that completely wild?" I respond to his outburst with a smile. Then, at last, we set off on our saunter around the homes of Granvin's fiddle players.

Within walking distance of Knut's red house lived a fiddle player and maker by the name of Håvard Kvandal (1910-2005). I was only able to meet him in the final year of his life, when he was 95 years old, but I am grateful for the opportunity. He was kind and witty, and lit up when he spoke about the old days. The tiny ochre-painted outhouse he used as his workshop was practically a music academy in itself, when one thought about all those who had set foot inside, and everything shared, repaired, and played within its walls.

After Kvanndal, Knut and I continue into Folkedal, where Knut himself grew up. Another notable fiddle player who lived here was Olav Sekse (1823-1896), known as "Folkedalen," whose most well-known tunes included "Folkedalen, "Personvrita," and "Seksaren." He was a good dancer, and in 1850 was invited by the famous violinist Ole Bull to play in Bergen during the opening season of Det Norske Theater, the first pure stage theater in Norway. Other than that, we know little about him. Such is the case for most of these old fiddle players. What we do know is that they were outstanding fiddlers, and may also have been great teachers. It's possible we might know what other professions they had outside of music, or where they lived, especially in the years when it was normal to change your surname after each farmstead one moved to or owned. Other than that, we only have a few morsels of information, like Olav Sekse's stint at Det Norske Theater. We know that Nils Rogdo from Sørfjorden went to America and never came back, that Rekveen from Voss was killed when someone poured lye into his beer, and that Ola Mosafinn once met Edvard Grieg and Ole Bull when they were visiting Lofthus. Little more.

We drive on to Eide, the heart of Granvin and home to many great fiddlers of ages past. Among them was Lars Røynstrand, who was not only an excellent fiddler but also a fiddle teacher, tailor, hunter, fisherman, farmer, storyteller, and clockmaker. We stop here to spend a little time on his farm, and we are met with Lars's great- great-grandchild. We are even allowed a peek at his old fiddle and sewing machine. Severin Kjerland (1867-1961) and his son, Anders (1900-1989), also lived in Eide. We pay a visit to their house and Anders's old workshop before driving toward Voss and the neighborhood of Vassenden in Øvre Granvin. This was the home of Eirik Medås (1769-1854), who ran a guesthouse and became the mentor of many talented, well-known fiddlers. It is strangely delightful to think that I and a great many others can still play the same notes and melodies that Medås used to play, even though he was born in 1769 and I in 1983.

We spend the whole day driving around these narrow green lanes, and Knut retells anecdotes about who lived where and who learned from whom, and where he used to play after school. After visiting the hamlets of Medås , Ystaas, Vindal, Selland, Prestgarden, and Spildo, among others, we finally end up on old Bulko farm, where the fiddle player Per Bulko (1797-1876) lived as a young boy. As Bulko marks the parish boundary into Voss, we give up here and turn back to Kvanndal, where I let Knut out of my car and thank him for the trip.

Back on the road to Bergen, cars rocket past me at breakneck speed. Not wise. The road beyond Kvanndal to Ålvik isn't built for that kind of driving. But it's tourist season. Big buses surround me in droves, filled with tour guides carrying microphones and barking out information from next to the driver's seat. I realize it's probably a good thing that so few people know about *all* of these hidden spots. Most people just zoom right past, and farms like Håstabø can remain the pearls they are, precious and alone.

Øvre Vassenden, Granvin in 1886, the home of fiddle player Eirik Medås.

Fiddle player Lars Røynstrand and his wife Anna Nilsdtr. Kollanes.

Fiddle player Olav Sekse, also known as "Folkedalen."

Olav Håstabø.

It walks and walks

and all the dead are with us

the dead too walk and walk

in us

walk and walk

everything walks and walks

the dead who are gone

the dead who are only almost gone

and everything walks and walks

and everything that exists

it walks and walks

the birds fly in the sky

the fish swim under the water

we walk and walk

everything walks and walks

Jon Fosse

(Translated by May-Brit Akerholm)

Erick Vrserie
10 1843

Fiddle player Eirik Medås, painted by Adolph Tidemand in 1843.

THE MASTER-STUDENT LINEAGE IN GRANVIN

Anved Storegraven (1729-1810)
Eirik Medås (1769-1854)
Otte Haukanes (1788-1847)
Eirik Selland (1797-1885)
Hans Selland (1821-1893)
Lars Røynstrand (1822-1899)
Olav Håstabø (1826-1899)
Severin Kjerland (1867-1961)
Anders Kjerland (1900-1989)
Knut Hamre (1952-)

THE MASTER'S MASTERS

THE FIRST MASTER
ANDERS KJERLAND
(1900-1989)

1964 | It is the 16th of May. Knut is twelve years old and cycling enthusiastically down the narrow lane leading from his home of Folkedal to Eide in Granvin. He is carrying his fiddle in his rucksack. If he were to cast a glance to either side while pedaling, his mind would be sent into spirals. At the edge of the mountain is a sudden 800-meter drop into the fjord. But today, Knut doesn't spare a thought for danger. He is almost beside himself. He whizzes into the center of Granvin, to the house of master fiddler Anders Kjerland, for the first time. The Sunday prior, after Knut finished playing at a gathering in the house of fiddle maker Håvard Kvandal, Anders had said: "You must come visit me." A few days later, Knut is finally on his way.

He arrives at Anders's red house in a place called Oppitun in Kjerland. Knut and Anders each take a stool to sit on in the tiny inbuilt terrace of his living room. Fiddles in hand, they gaze out on the little village. None of Anders's children is at home, only his wife Anna, who is preparing something for them to eat.

Anders plays through an old tune three times, called "Bruremarsj etter Olav Bergsland." Knut watches his hands, listening closely and mimicking his notes and finger work. Anders stops and listens to Knut play on his own, making sure he has everything down. Most of it is okay, with the exception of a few strokes of his bow, which Anders corrects. Then Knut plays the whole tune again, with Anders listening. Anders proclaims his satisfaction with Knut's fiddling and asks him to come again next week.

Over the next decade, until 1974, he meets with Anders a regular basis, learning everything possible about fiddle music's tunes, techniques, and history.

LEARNING TO PLAY
IS LIKE LEARNING A LANGUAGE

Knut followed his new teacher's orders, making the trip to his house—whether by bus, bike, or foot—every week after school. Fiddle music came naturally to him, due largely to the fact he had heard the tunes Anders played many times before. All of them "sat right in his ear." If Knut didn't learn a tune quickly the first time round, Anders would grow impatient. He would pace around the room, whistling the tunes and gesturing with his arms how each stroke of the bow should go. It was best to take lots of short trips to see Anders, rather than long ones few and far between.

"Anders told stories with his fiddle," Knut tells me, "and I can recall his playing as far back as my mind can remember. As a boy, when I first heard this music, I was enchanted. Despite all the students and peers Anders had visiting him, I still believe he most enjoyed playing by himself and, not least, telling stories. That might have been when he was at his very best. Every story he ever told still lives on inside of me. He had a dry, cutting sense of humor. One of his stories goes like this: Nils Eide (known as 'Tråen') once sat playing his fiddle while his brother Eirik was fooling around with a revolver. Suddenly there was an accident, and Eirik let loose a shot that went whistling through Nils's playing hand, mid-melody...but the fiddle—it was fine!"

When Knut was growing up, Anders Kjerland was the best fiddle player in all of Hardanger. He had won national folk music competitions of the highest degree, played at countless dances, weddings, and other celebrations, and even held concerts together with the great pianist Geirr Tveitt and poet Olav H. Hauge, who read his own poetry. Anders was also adored in his hometown and never refused anyone who asked him to play.

Many people were well-versed in Hardanger folk music when Knut was growing up, but Anders was the one man who knew it all. He had an awe-inspiring knowledge of the history of fiddle tunes and fiddlers up and down the entire fjord. He was peerless in his knowledge of both Hardanger's traditional fiddle music (*slåttemusikk*) and its repertoire of old-time dances (*gamaldansmusikk*), a staggering 500-600 pieces in total. He couldn't read notes, so he had to keep it all in his head. To make sure he never forgot any, he kept a small book in which he wrote down the first finger positions of each tune.

"Anders was the undisputed expert on Hardanger's fiddle music. If someone learned a fiddle piece from one of the other fiddlers in Granvin, they would always show it to Anders, and I had to check everything I learned from them with him, too."

Was he a great teacher? I ask him.

"No, but nevertheless, there was no doubt he was a master of the art."

So why do you think he wasn't a good teacher when he was such a great fiddler?

"Anders's main drawback was that he had never had any difficulties learning to play the Hardanger fiddle. His fingering technique was second to none, and he had mastered it on his own, without a great amount of trouble or analysis. That was why it was no use asking him for any advice on technique. He had never needed to think about it, and so he lacked the words to explain in a smart, pedagogical way. On the other hand, Anders was exceptionally knowledgeable about precisely how each tune should be played. It was as though they had been nailed right into his head. And although he didn't enjoy teaching, he was passionate about ensuring that not a single fiddle tune would die with him. There was no talk of any kind of payment, or exchange of favors, for any of these sessions with him. He was well aware that back then he was the only person who had a complete command of the Hardanger tradition, and that in the 1960s people weren't exactly lining up to learn about the subject. Quite the opposite."

Maybe it was a good thing you didn't get easy answers from your master?

"I think it was both healthy and necessary. Otherwise I would have become a soft student. In terms of technique, however, there were many things it would have been helpful to know about earlier than I did. But I found it all out later anyway. You can't learn everything from just one master."

Anders and Knut rarely allocated a specific time for their appointments. Calendars didn't exist in Granvin back then. If Anders wasn't home when Knut got there, he was nearly always in the nearby carpentry workshop where he worked during the day. And if Anders didn't have time for him, Knut could always learn a tune or two from one of the other workers at the workshop. After all, every one of them played the Hardanger fiddle, too.

"For me, learning to play the Hardanger fiddle has never felt like hard work. On the contrary, it has always been a kind of game. When I was growing up in Granvin, even if people didn't know how to play the fiddle, they would always be able to hum or whistle the tunes."

It must have made your education much easier, I think. The way that fiddle music was a natural part of your daily life as well as of those around you. When I was young I only ever heard you play one session a week.

"Yes, precisely! The violinist Yehudi Menuhin has written about his encounters with various musicians from the gypsy community in Romania. There, he heard young children perform violin music more exquisite than the playing of countless adult classical musicians who had spent their entire lives in practice rooms, training to master the art form. Why is that? Probably because these children were learning to play the fiddle as though they were learning to speak. And if someone has been learning a language or a skill since birth, then it is impossible to stop it from flowing naturally. This is how I have experienced fiddle playing."

Severin Kjerland and his grandson Knut A. Kjerland on the pump organ, playing at a wedding in Granvin around 1957.

Knut explains that Anders Kjerland was obsessed with developing good fingering techniques, a broad knowledge of fiddle tunes, and playing every single bow stroke by the book, as it were. He saw a tight, sharp rhythm as important, and every tune needed to make you want to dance to it. A *rull* was a *rull* and that was that. Anders also spoke at length about the bow's narrative voice. He loved to conjure up imagery when explaining these things to Knut. He might point out that a piece needed a comma somewhere, or a full stop to suggest a kind of pause, and so on. And all these rhythmic devices came from the bowing hand.

"Looking back, it was a bit strange, because even though he played with a long classical bow, he would only ever use a short segment of the middle of the bow, keeping his strokes short and snappy. This was the complete opposite bowing technique to that of Halldor Meland, who was Anders Kjerland's fiddling mentor and a great inspiration for many others of his generation. Anders's own bowing technique likely came from his father, Severin Kjerland, who also happened to be his foremost teacher. Yet it could also have stemmed from Ola Mosafinn, a fiddler from Voss, who visited the Kjerland household on numerous occasions."

Anders believed a good melody to be invaluable. He didn't like it when people messed with a good thing, adding too many notes or embellishments. It was far better to peel away layers than to add them. But most important of all was the tune itself, and your choice of fiddle could affect this. Hence why Anders had intentionally laid his hands on fiddles with a warm, dark, and mellow sound color. During Anders's childhood, the norm was to have fiddles tuned to A (440 Hz) or lower, with thick gut strings.

"These days, this has gone completely out of fashion, with a few exceptions, such as yourself. To some extent it's possible to create a beautiful tone based on your technique with any instrument, but I think this skill largely comes down to something you either do or don't already have. But the instrument itself can play a big role. For this reason, Anders tuned his fiddle to a slightly lower pitch to produce a warmer sound—either the concert pitch of A or A#—instead of each string tuned up a whole tone or more, which is today's standard among Hardanger fiddlers. The fact that most fiddle players tune their instruments higher than they used to is probably more for practical than aesthetic reasons. Sadly, most fiddlers opt for volume over a beautiful sound. I also think that over the past thirty years, these group performances popular among fiddlers nowadays have done their part in turning the A-string up to B into the norm. Of course, these fiddle groups needed to find a common pitch for tuning their fiddles. The same can be said of how students are all taught in cultural institutions."

Midsummer wedding in Granvin.
The fiddle player on the right is the young Anders Kjerland.

SEEKING THE MYSTICAL

1974 | Knut, who had just turned twenty-two, arrived at the national *kappleik* in Oppdal. As usual, he intended to take part in the competition while listening to, and potentially meeting, all the great fiddle players gathered there: Torleiv Bolstad, Hans W. Brimi, Torleiv Bjørgum, and Ola Bøe, among others. Folk music was in the air—in those days *kappleik* were the only venues available to play and to hear good playing. Few knew who Knut Hamre was.

Knut performed two tunes in the gymnasium of the school where the *kappleik* was being held. The atmosphere was positively electric. The crowd was packed and people were scrambling up the gymnastics equipment to catch a view of the performance. As Knut brought his final note to a close, the people cried out for more. He left the stage dripping with sweat—shaking, dazed, and happy. A fiddle player from Lom, the great Hans W. Brimi, was waiting behind the curtain to relieve Knut of his fiddle before he collapsed backstage. Knut remembers nothing after that. Only that it felt boundlessly fantastic to play.

No one that day had expected Knut to play above and beyond all of his heroes to win the *kappleik*. No fiddle player as young as him had ever ranked first at the national *kappleik* before. Reactions were both positive and negative. His fans celebrated; his rivals' eyes turned dark. The daily news program, NRK Dagsrevyen, broadcast the year's winner on live TV. This was followed by press interviews. Who was this man who had come out of nowhere to beat all the old favorites? How could someone so young play so uniquely? With such rhythmic ease? So improvised and free? So beautifully and mysteriously? With endless ornaments and dreamlike bowing?

Just who was this Knut Hamre from Granvin, who turned away from his audience, covering his face with his long hair?

Although Anders Kjerland's tuition bore fruit for Knut, his trips to Anders's house became less and less frequent between 1970 and 1974. After that there was a gap of many years. The reason for this was simple. They each developed their own, differing attitudes toward their discipline and toward musical expression. As Knut entered his early twenties, he felt a growing need to rebel against this "all-knowing figure." He needed to do something different with his music, and could no longer go on playing exactly like Anders Kjerland.

"What's more, after a while I began to long for a more spiritual dimension within my music. Because of this longing, I started to seek out other masters, such as Bjarne Herrefoss and Eivind Mo. All this came to me by instinct, like an inner compass. Yet I never truly broke away from Hardanger's traditional fiddle music (*slåttemusikk*). On the contrary, the farther I distanced myself from Anders and the other Granvin fiddlers, the closer and more connected I felt to the music itself. I was also feeling fed up with all their expectations and pressure. After all, many people considered me to be my generation's sole heir to the folk music tradition in Hardanger. So I think they saw it as an abuse of trust when I had to distance myself."

Did you feel done with Anders's mentorship?

"I was in some ways, but wasn't in others, precisely because of the way I felt closer to the tradition when I broke from the many unwritten codes within it. When I was young, I gobbled up Anders's repertoire. Everything he said was gospel. My tunnel vision toward his playing was a big help back then in terms of learning the craft itself. I have relied on the craft I learned from

Anders throughout my whole working life as a fiddle player. Perhaps this explains why I have always felt so free to express myself when playing. I know that whatever I play, I have these sturdy foundations, this craft on my side."

Throughout the length of Knut's time spent under Anders Kjerland, his education never changed, working in precisely the same way at age twelve as at twenty-two. Now that Knut had broken the codes that needed to be broken, he was ready to move forward.

"In fact, Anders played the same way throughout his whole professional life. You can hear it in recordings of him from various periods in his life. Later, it hit me that this might have been due to a modern classic zeitgeist at the time, since both Sigbjørn Bernhoft Osa and Lars Skjervheim did the same. Perhaps they thought of each tune as more of a fixed work or composed piece of music, and so they should be performed in the same way every time."

Or maybe Anders's music was more a matter of routine?

"For Anders, music was something both sacred and mundane. His music served a function and was an important part of his daily life. But it was without any mystery. Its inexplicable or spiritual features weren't an issue. His music was down to earth, without lofty words and gestures. I must have offended him greatly when I started to interpret music differently to how he thought I should. I know he felt disappointed in me, and regarded me as a poor trustee of the tradition."

What was different in the way you played?

"Well, nothing, to tell the truth. If a fiddler comes from Hardanger, then they will play in a somewhat similar way, despite the idiosyncrasies of each player."

Yet when I hear recordings of you and Anders, it is almost impossible to believe that you studied under him. So there must have been something you did differently?

"Of course, in concrete terms, I improvised much more than Anders would ever have done. I also used more ornaments, applied a different bowing, loosened up tight rhythms, and so forth. But as I saw it, I always did so with a common aesthetic that I shared with him and everyone else in Hardanger. If I played differently from them, then it came from a place inside of me that I wasn't aware of. This was why I struggled to understand why so many people reacted so strongly toward my playing."

But perhaps it was more controversial that you were praised at the national kappleik *in Oppdal for playing something that Anders and other fiddle players in his circle didn't approve of?*

"I was awfully naïve in those days, and truly thought that everyone would be pleased when someone played the fiddle well. I wasn't at all bothered about winning *kappleikar* so early in my twenties. I just wanted somewhere to perform. Folk music festivals and the like didn't exist yet, so the only way to play in front of a crowd was at a *kappleik*. Yet the main issue with all this was that it was undermining Anders's position as a fiddle player far more than by me just being a poor heir to the tradition. By becoming the youngest person to ever win the national *kappleik*, I was whittling away at the established rules about how people should play the fiddle. I obviously shouldn't have won. Although I played well for my age, and perhaps the bowing of my older competitors might have been a bit shaky, their performances clearly had a far more mature musical expressivity than that of my young self. This meant I had even damaged the reputation and position of the national *kappleik* as the highest arena to assess and define what counted as excellent fiddle playing. They had no way of measuring *dåm*[4] (soul), which is why they ranked more highly any playing that was outstanding in terms of technique. And that's how it is at *kappleikar* still."

As Knut was making headway as a fiddle player, Anders was having difficulties being open-minded about his playing. Yet the conflict never truly sparked between Knut and Anders, but between all those on the margins of the debate, who felt they needed to take sides. There were never any open discussions, just a whole lot of bickering in the "backroom."

"From that moment on there were countless opinions flying around Hardanger and the folk music community about how I should or shouldn't be playing my fiddle. Folks have a knack for forming cliques that stand either for or against something. It all eventually became so unbearable that I had to avoid both sides for a long time."

Didn't all this make you sad? If you had reacted like this toward me when I did well in something, then I would have been really upset.

"Of course! But this is unfortunately the standard reaction most people will have. I don't find it difficult to understand the psychology behind it. The opposition I faced gradually became like a confirmation of what I was doing, that it was solid and something new. How else could it give rise to such heated debate? Nowadays, there isn't much that can surprise me when it comes to the human psyche. But it still makes me just as sad when I find a new depth people will sink to in order to inflict harm on one another."

How did you cope with all this opposition at such a young age?

"Very badly. The more opposition I met, particularly in the late 1970s and early 80s, the more important it became for me to win at *kappleikar*—to prove that I had something to give. But trying to show that you're the 'best' has nothing to do with music. I may have silenced a few tongues by winning so many times in so few years, but for me personally, it was an extremely short-lived pleasure."

The truth is we're probably eager to be generous toward others, as long as they don't threaten our own position.

"It can take a lifetime to master true generosity. It requires maturity and a mind free of any domineering ego."

Perhaps all this between you and Anders came about more through bad chemistry and communication than any issues about status.

"That was the true seed that pushed us apart. I had, and still have, a great sense of unrest that never goes away. Anders never understood this feeling, and was probably baffled that I couldn't just play it exactly how I had learned it. But I remember that Anders used to pose the same sort of questions to his own teacher, Halldor Meland. Why did he always have to keep changing these fiddle tunes all the time? Adding to them, and so forth? For me, the answer was simple: Halldor just got bored. And if Halldor Meland could get bored, then maybe it was okay for me to get bored, too? So I started to ask myself: Should I play 'Flatabøen' the same way every time? No, I shouldn't. If I had to, then I would stop playing it altogether, which would be a shame, given that it is so beautiful. This was why I started adding layers and re-arranging different tunes, improvising on them and such. Many older fiddle players in Granvin were fascinated when they heard this, but at the same time felt unable to accept this twenty-something who had no respect at all for his sources! Today I am grateful for the way I become bored so quickly, and for all the opposition I've faced, which just gave me more energy. If you want to go far as an artist, then challenge is an essential driving force."

But did Anders seriously manage to play perfectly by the book his entire life? Sounds like an impossible task to me.

"When he played, Anders Kjerland saw himself as retelling a story he had heard from his own sources. A human mind is rarely constant, and neither was Anders's brain, despite its unbelievable catalog of fiddle tunes. If you hear a recording of his father, Severin Kjerland, you'll hear many differences from Anders's own rendition of the same tune, at the very least in tonality. Anders played a lot of one-string pieces, for example, yet in the notations of Sjur Håstabø ('The Nock') who came before him, there is obvious use of *bordunspel* (bowing two strings simultaneously) in some of these tunes. Anders Kjerland was a man of many contradictions. He could happily criticize something one second, then praise it loudly a moment later."

So why do you think that Severin and Anders played so differently, even though they were father and son?

"For the simple reason that they were two different types of people who grew up in different times and had different external influences. It's important to remember that Severin was born in 1867 and Anders in 1910. The fact that Anders's playing was closer to equal temperament than his father's probably stems from the early start the younger man had in playing *gamaldansmusikk* at dances. There, he would play accompanied by equally tempered instruments such as the pump organ, the accordion, and the piano.[5] Severin never did this. Geirr Tveitt once bought a piano and donated it to the local folk music union in Hardanger, so that they would have a good instrument to accompany them while they played their Hardanger fiddles. They put this piano in Granvin's cultural center."

I guarantee Geirr Tveitt meant well by this, but it does strike me as strange. Particularly when I think about how obsessed he was in his own music with these age-old microtones and different modes.

"Yes, you could say that. But another thing that definitely influenced Anders Kjerland's generation was the radio. When Anders was growing up, it was becoming a normal piece of furniture in most living rooms and so it was natural to hear lots of music other than Hardanger fiddling, which would come to have a profound effect on the tonality of folk music."

THE SECOND PHASE OF LEARNING

In 1984, Knut started having sessions with Anders again, and this time they would continue right up until Anders's death in 1989. By this point, Anders had probably realized that if this music was going to survive, he had to share it with someone who was dedicated enough to learn all Hardanger had to offer. Anders was both touched and taken aback when he understood that Knut actually had a good grasp of Hardanger's tradition. In their prolonged time apart, Knut had spent time listening to recordings of such other fiddle players from Granvin as Håvard Kvandal, Einar Spildo, and Kristoffer Kjerland. He had even visited them all in person to learn their music straight from the source.

"I used my final years with Anders to perfect tunes and teach myself any that were still new to me, for example those that Anders had forgotten he could play. Now there were also more discussions about the art form itself, in which I would pose to him completely new types of questions. He had become wiser in his old age. Our communication became freer, too, not to mention the fact that there was more mutual respect. In both my first and final lesson with Anders, he never ceased to offer up lively and incredible tales of the fjord's history and fiddle players."

Did you consider him a good friend, and not just a master?

"No, there was never any close friendship or personal bond between us. This was all about the art. But I never felt any sense of lack for it. I am humbly grateful for everything I could learn from Anders. He has been my solid foundation and fiddle icon throughout my entire life."

THE SECOND MASTER
BJARNE HERREFOSS
(1931-2002)

1968 | All of a sudden, Bjarne Herrefoss is standing in the doorway of the old café in Sandven. Knut is sixteen and has taken the trip from Granvin to Bø alone to witness the local *kappleik*. He doesn't know anyone, and sits all by himself on a bench up against the café wall. It's bustling. The room is roaring with laughter, music, and conversation. Steam rises from bowls of hot stew, and people in sweaty *bunads*[6] are clinking their glasses together. The sound of fiddles is everywhere as instruments are passed over tables from one player to another. Some listen, others chat.

Bjarne says nothing as his big, tall frame towers in the café entrance, clad in a black suit. He gazes around and spots a scared and shy Knut sitting alone at the far end of the room. Knut recognizes Bjarne Herrefoss from his pictures, but knows his playing style even better from the *Folkemusikkhalvtimen*[7] (Folk Music Half-Hour) radio program. But he has never met him. Knut has a burning desire to hear Bjarne play, and feels almost paralyzed by his yearning for the music. Their eyes meet, and without hesitation Bjarne crosses the floor between them and sticks out his hand: "Bjarne Herrefoss." He then sits down next to Knut on the bench, takes his hand, and holds it for a long time. He says nothing. There they sit, hand in hand, until Bjarne bolts to his feet, grabs his half-opened fiddle case, and leaves with his fiddle's silk covering dangling along the floor.

AN UNSPOKEN TEACHING

"I will play life. For life we know nothing about," Bjarne once said before playing at a café during Geilo's national *kappleik* in 1969. A year had passed since he walked through the doors of the old Sandven Café. When Knut heard him play for the first time, Bjarne's music was everything he had hoped for, his tone fragile and filled with melancholy and warmth.

In 1972, Knut began his mentorship under Bjarne. They met at *kappleikar* and spent a great deal of time on the phone or visiting each other's houses. Bjarne worked at power stations in both Aurland and Odda, so he spent much of his life traveling up and down the Hardangerfjord. They would meet either at Knut's home or at the house of the fiddle maker Håvard Kvandal. In 1975, Bjarne moved to Skafså near Dalen in Telemark, and from then on theirs became a more "formal" teacher-student relationship with frequent meetings. Their mentorship was never structured or clearly defined, but after a while it settled into more of a routine. This lasted for about thirty years, until Bjarne's death.

"He liked to sit in his living room when I visited him in Skafså, smoking Petterøe's Blå cigarettes and staring out the window. As a rule, little was said. Then, without warning, he would jump to his feet, snatch up his fiddle from the table, and start playing away in the kitchen for a long period of time, while I stayed in the living room. Communication between us consisted more of strange little signals than actual conversation. In social situations, he would sometimes get completely lost inside his own thoughts, drifting off and fading away. Then all of a sudden, a look would light up his face and he would break into a warm smile, until—just as quickly—he would drift off again."

He does sound mercifully different.

"Yes, and thank goodness for it! He was quite an oddball, and was always enveloped in this totally unique vibe. I was often bewitched by the strange things he came out with, such as: 'Do you want to join me on a day that doesn't exist?'"

What linked the two of you together?

"The unspoken. And through the unspoken, I learned so much

more from Bjarne than anyone else I have met. To be honest, I never learned a single fiddle tune from him. Yet he was always my foremost master."

Bjarne Herrefoss grew up in Seljordshei and was an incredibly gifted fiddler. Like Anders Kjerland, he learned the music of his own rich folk music community. He could never recall where he had heard or learned a tune, and never learned anything note for note. He didn't have the patience for it, and always said: "I don't play fiddle tunes; I play music!" Whenever Bjarne and Knut met, their encounters might happily have gone on for several days. They spent their time playing for one another, listening to recordings, reading poetry, debating issues, or just sitting in silence together. But when they did converse, it was usually around questions about the music itself. For example: What happens to the music when your mood changes? If something was missing in Knut's expression, Bjarne might tell him: "There aren't enough clouds in your music." Or, if he liked it: "Now roses are growing out of your fingers." When he thought Knut was playing especially well, he might suddenly burst out: "I just died!" Bjarne always spoke his mind without hesitation. When it came to art, his criticism often came across as harsh. But he was never stubborn, and changed his opinions constantly.

"With Bjarne, you had to forget about concrete answers or recipes, and it was never easy to come to terms with that. But if you stepped outside your own boundaries, he would politely interrupt and tell you: 'You must be where you must be.'"

BJARNE-TUNES

As a fiddler, Bjarne was always yearning for the limelight. He was never self-analytical and never listened to recordings of himself in order to improve or alter his playing. What was done was done. Music should be spontaneous. At times he would play fiddle music that was reasonably close to the original, but in the right state of mind would sometimes venture out on lengthy improvisations.

"The fiddler Olav Øyaland told me that he once timed Bjarne playing 'Fjellrosa' at a *kappleik*. The piece is supposed to last around three or four minutes if you play it through twice, which is the norm for fiddle players. But that day, Bjarne played for a whopping twenty-one minutes! The quality of Bjarne's improvisations varied greatly. If he wasn't what he called 'soaring in the moment,' it might very well collapse into nothing."

He strikes me as a very free fiddle player.

"Yes, in every way. If he felt the need to change the form of the tune, or only play certain parts he liked, then he would do so. In his day, of course, it was unheard of to do such things, and it still isn't common now, either. He was the same with the names of each tune. Once at a *kappleik* he started mixing up the name 'Floketjønn' with 'Håvards sorg,' another well-known tune from Telemark. The latter title ('Håvard's Grief') probably fit better with his state of mind at the time, so he changed it."

Most of what Bjarne Herrefoss played was original, especially in his clear and distinctive ornamentation of a tune. He often used his little finger to elicit minor trills and variations, as was rare among fiddle players. Performing such snappy, precise movements with your little finger is exceptionally demanding.

Suspending his strings closer to the fingerboard and tuning his fiddle to a higher pitch also helped to produce these bright, deft embellishments. The grace notes he worked into the main melody were slower and more searching than to-the-point, thus producing an almost pained sound, like wailing. What's more, he had an outstanding grasp of the fiddle in terms of technique. He could make microscopic variations in his bowing that would become all the more prominent when he changed the amount of pressure he applied to his bow. He might begin by holding back, then slowly let loose, particularly with his upstroke, thereby able to draw in his audience in a totally unique way. He always loved to surprise listeners by pretending a tune was about to end before suddenly launching back into it with a renewed vigor that kept him going on and on. He would also repeat and improvise tiny variations in the melody as if he were in a kind of meditative state. Sometimes his variations were so minute that you needed a trained ear to hear them. But the effect was strongly emotive.

These "Bjarne-tunes" have become a genre of their own, haven't they?

"Yes, he has claimed a certain repertoire for himself. It isn't very big, only around 50 to 60 tunes in all. He spent his whole life changing their names and contents. Nearly all of them were in the tuning of what we call *oppstilt bass* (tuned-up bass), in which the fiddle's fourth and lowest string is tuned up a whole step from G to A, so that the fiddle's tuning becomes A-D-A-E. On a few occasions I heard him play in *nedstilt bass* (down-tuned bass, or G-D-A-E), but never in any other fiddle tuning (*scordatura*), despite how captivated he was by the ways a tune might change color accordingly. He could easily have done more with this technique if he had used a wider variety of the twenty-six different tunings and more we have in Norwegian fiddle music. One of his more concrete decisions was to considerably loosen the hair of his bow to produce a larger sound and broader tone. This was because if the hairs of the bow are wound too tightly, then despite producing a more forthright tone that would carry better through a room, you might also get a sharper sound. I have since learned that many of the old Hardanger fiddlers were much the same as Bjarne, and settled on loosening their bows."

Bjarne's playing style consisted of long, dramatic bow strokes. He was not so concerned with the rhythmic qualities of the music. During his improvisations, he might completely dissolve a steady rhythm and break up its pulse like a jazz musician. In fact, many people believed Bjarne was a jazz musician at heart. In terms of pure aesthetics, he was first and foremost interested in a warm, rich tone, since he believed that a tone reflected one's human qualities. He believed those who produced a good tone to be warm, beautiful people, while a cold tone came from those beset by stressed and troubled hearts.

"Thinking along these lines can actually be rather flawed. Because you can also produce a good tone by working extremely hard on your technique, as in the case of Anders Kjerland. Yet I am convinced that you need a big heart to make big music."

CLIMAX ON STAGE

"First I knocked the audience off their feet. Then I was playing for God!" This was Bjarne's own reply to the Setesdal fiddle player, Hallvard T. Bjørgum, when asked how he at a *kappleik* in Porsgrunn some years before had managed to make his playing soar through the roof.

"When it came to focusing your mind on a single point, Bjarne had no equals. This is the principal reason why his playing was able to elevate itself beyond what was deemed normal. The times when his stage performances really hit home were when the bridge between Bjarne and his audience became utterly open. In those instances he produced something powerful, a warm and sincere feeling of generosity. Sometimes he cried while he played. Yet unless everything was perfect for Bjarne, both mentally and physically, his playing was rather average. He knew he had a great power inside of him, but that it would only come forth if he kept the channel open."

I've even heard that many actors and other artists have tried to seek him out, in the hopes of learning the secrets of entering into this state of "soaring."

"In that case I would hazard a guess that Bjarne would give them a clean and simple response: 'You must be where you are.' But I knew Bjarne spent a lot of time together with the fiddler Gjermund Haugen, who was known to have the same gift. It's rather improbable to assume that Bjarne didn't learn something from Haugen."

What kind of techniques do you think he used to tap into these states of superior concentration?

"I remember him once saying, 'I play a long time before I play.' I remember how he was able to bring all his thoughts into line, and shut out everything other than the music he wanted to tap into. He would prepare by spending time alone, too, just him and his fiddle, without speaking. At times he might permit himself the company of a few select others, but only, in his own words, if they gave him energy instead of stealing it away. What's more, he preferred to have a good amount of time to prepare, and so would always arrive at the venue early. He wasn't keen on tuning his fiddle onstage, because he believed this disrupted both himself and his audience. He avoided playing long concerts, too. His ideal concert consisted

of seven to eight drawn-out tunes, divided into two sets with a long pause between. If he felt like he wasn't in the right state of mind, he would stop playing long before he was supposed to. I think Bjarne played at his best when a certain melancholia rose up inside him, in conjunction with his deep state of concentration. This allowed him to enter a more permeable, sensitive state."

Knut explains that there was no use asking Bjarne Herrefoss to play something specific. It annoyed Bjarne greatly. When it came to the written and unwritten rules of what was right and what was wrong, Bjarne accepted no conditions. All the usual prattle of the folk music community about where each tune came from, who learned what from whom, who had the best fiddles, who was good at playing and who less so—you never heard Bjarne breathing a word about any of it. If you asked Bjarne where he had learned a tune, the standard answer was: 'An old guy was sitting outside the Skarsmo village shop near Odda. I heard him playing it as I walked past.'

"This was why so many in the folk music community doubted his abilities. Bjarne was always controversial, and rarely sought approval or pats on the head. He received a great deal of criticism from his peers, but was naturally held in high esteem by many of them, too."

Did the negative criticism have an effect on him?

"Yes and no. As I understand it, it saddened him, but he also didn't give a damn."

So Bjarne wasn't worried about looking after a tradition?

"He was searching for the unique quality within music, rather than caring about any references to antiquity. Bjarne would

say that our lives should be led by our music, not the other
way around. One could hear echoes from his sources and he
did inherit the general characteristics of the Hardanger fiddle
tradition. But he let other people worry about the details. It was
simply the way he was so free that became a true inspiration for
me."

Did he ever get lonely from ostracizing himself like this?

"He was an outcast for much of his life, something he both
liked and disliked. Bjarne was a paradox. He could be happy in
a small room with a handful of people or on a humongous stage
in front of an uncountable audience. He didn't feel as though
he belonged anywhere, and in many environments felt excluded
from 'respectable company.' But he could often resolve issues
with his music rather than his words. I recall one occasion when
Bjarne and I were visiting Selfjord's famous fiddle player, Eivind
Mo. Eivind had a sharp tongue, and on this occasion he had just
finished listening to some recordings on the radio of a collection
of fiddle players, including Bjarne. Eivind wasn't too keen on
the recordings, and piped up in his thin, grating voice: 'That
recording was diabolically talentless.' In response, Bjarne picked
up his fiddle, played a heavenly beautiful rendition of 'Gaute
Navarsgard,' then plonked it back in its case without saying a
word. There were tears streaming down Eivind's face.

"It strikes me as strange that Eivind spoke so harshly that
day. I know that he actually harbored a deep respect for Bjarne's
playing style, and would even use recordings of him at courses
for judges before taking part at *kappleikar* to demonstrate a
playing style that was complete and *dåmerikt* (soulful and deep).
Rather ironically, after he had experienced so much exclusion
and insult, a group of Bjarne's supporters set up a fan club as
well as their own *spelemannslag* (fiddle association) in his name.
But he didn't take kindly to it at all. He firmly opposed any

form of one-sided idolatry. Sometimes, wondrous occurrences simply happen. And so, when people can't tame the unknown, they cultivate it instead, to convince themselves of being able to maintain some element of control."

"I HAVE DIED MANY TIMES"

Bjarne Herrefoss knew he was never going to be an old man. He had lived hard and burnt the candle at both ends. Because of his divorce and poor financial situation, Bjarne was facing hard times toward the end of the 1960s. He disappeared for a long time, roughing it on his own with no house, income, or family of five gnawing on his conscience. Then, sometime between 1970 and 1972, Bjarne's wife-to-be, Vesla, came into his life. From that point on, everything was a lot easier. He continued to struggle with mental issues throughout his life, and a combination of alcohol abuse and factory work—which he hated—led to serious mental and physical ailments. Set routines simply didn't agree with Bjarne. Anything that stood in the way of his freedom, whether family or work, was unbearable. It was the same with his fiddle music. There were to be no systems, and he was completely unyielding to any obstacles. The most important thing of all was his freedom.

"It can't have been easy for those around him to understand such a unique and sensitive mind. But he was practically inclined when he wanted to be, and enjoyed fishing, berry picking, and woodcarving. He could also be extremely pedantic, neat, and organized. He could be pretty hopeless at all that, too. Food was often burnt at Bjarne's house. He saw no worth in material goods, not even fiddles. Most of his life he didn't even own a Hardanger fiddle, and had to borrow one from others around him."

Bjarne would sometimes end up completely beside himself when Knut left him, and this only grew more and more intense the longer their relationship lasted. He had no filter on his emotions whatsoever, which just as well led to him to produce phenomenal music. His heart was completely open, for better or worse.

"I once brought along one of my students, Åse Teigland, to visit Bjarne. I recall how utterly raw and intense his playing was that day. Then, in the evening, Bjarne and I took a hike through the woods. He spoke with the trees, asking them how long they had stood there, about what they had seen and experienced. The next day, once we had finished breakfast and were making ready to leave, he had a complete breakdown. He sobbed and sobbed, totally unable to bear the fact that we were going to spend time apart.

"Another time we spent a few days playing and playing, and by the end Bjarne didn't want me to leave. As I stepped out the door he came after me, playing through the door, and out on the grass in front of his house at Skafså. As I got into my car he just stood there before the open sky, and the rain came pouring down on him and on his fiddle. He didn't notice the downpour at all. He just kept playing as I drove off."

Bjarne and Knut had each experienced a similar fate. They were both born as identical twins and had lost their twin brothers shortly after birth. Bjarne believed that he had been forced to absorb his dead brother's soul, which was why he had experienced such difficulty in his life, because of the pain of bearing two souls in one body. He was never a religious person, but believed he could draw energy from nature and the never-ending cycles of the world. Bjarne was hardly an intellectual, but had an understanding of many things that seemed hidden and inexplicable to others—the result of his unusually keen intuition. He also shared a special connection with animals. He had a remarkable way of speaking to the birds that lived around his house. They would come and alight on his arms, eating seeds out of the palm of his hand.

"I'll never forget the summer of 1975, when we were at a *kappleik* together in Fagernes. In the early hours of the morning, as I lay asleep in my tent, Bjarne woke me up. He was holding a tiny little white hare in his hand. He had found it while on an evening stroll through the woods."

What was the most important lesson you learned from Bjarne Herrefoss?

"Unrestrained generosity. Something you are utterly dependent on if you want to make music that is pure and true. What makes Bjarne stand out from many others who share similar qualities is that he managed to put his generosity into practice, in life as well as on the stage. Actions and words went hand in hand, and I never heard him utter a single harsh word about another human being. The way he offered up his music without holding back impressed me the whole time he was alive. He only did so by scaling down his own worth as an individual. He had no hidden motives, and played straight from the heart without expecting anything in return. Like he always used to say: 'Give all you have, and you'll get it all back twofold.'"

THE THIRD MASTER
OLAV H. HAUGE
(1908-1994)

1994 | One cold and clear morning in May, Knut was rung up by Bodil, Olav H. Hauge's wife, who told him: "Olav would like you to come to the house. He would like to bid you farewell." Knut jumped into his car right away and drove all the way from Folkedal to Rossvoll in Ulvik, to the farm with the apple trees standing ready to blossom, and the red house where Olav had lived his entire adult life. Olav had been in a bad way throughout the winter, and was now simply waiting for the sun and the spring to return one last time. Knut could almost see it happening with his naked eye, the blood flowing slower and slower through that old body's veins. When Knut entered the room, Olav sat hunched over in his bed, his legs crossed and a pillow behind his back. He was wrapped in a blanket and his emaciated body had sunk into itself. Between his hollow cheeks and shaggy beard, the only thing left of his face were those big, intense brown eyes.

"When I laid eyes on him, I thought to myself: Now you finally look like the people your inner self has been conversing with your entire life. An old Chinese wise man. A monk. A Bedouin of the desert. At last, you can 'sail away into another world' and be with your own kind."

Olav reached out his long arm and took Knut's hand. "Thanks for everything, Knut."

"No," Knut replied. "Thank you."

Then they sat together in silence until eventually Knut stood up, closed the door behind him, and drove home.

The next night, Olav was dead.

ON THE EAGLE'S TUSSOCK

1961 | Knut is nine years old, standing down by the fjord side in Folkedal, tapping his finger three times on the window of his friend, Agnar Folkedal. The cold December air frosts his breath as Knut peers inside, misting up the windowpane. Three raps is the secret code to signal that Knut is outside. Agnar, who is two years older than Knut, refuses to open the door unless he hears those three taps. People make him nervous and he doesn't like company, but the two boys enjoy getting together to read, daydream, and listen to the radio.

Today they are taking the bus to Granvin, then the train onto Voss, in order to pop into the bookshop there. They spend every Sunday listening to the radio program *Ønskediktet* (The Chosen Poem) and have recently become obsessed with a new poet who gave a reading from his new poetry collection, *På Ørnetuva* (On the Eagle's Tussock). The poet's name is Olav H. Hauge, from the nearby parish of Ulvik.

It's bitterly cold in Voss, yet bursting with life. Every street and shop window is decorated for Christmas. In Knut's pocket is every last penny of his savings. Back home he has twenty loyal hens who have laid a grand haul of eggs through the autumn, for which his neighbors have rewarded him generously. At the Ullestad bookshop they purchase the poetry collection *På Ørnetuva,* which they intend to share between them. Then they go into a café to eat some cakes while Agnar impersonates Olav's voice and reading style, as heard on the radio. He's diabolically good at it, and Knut laughs until he can laugh no more.

MEETING THE POET

Knut has always enjoyed being around books. As a little boy, he would often sub for his teacher at the public library in Folkedal. There, he would leaf through books containing the greatest Norwegian poets, such as Tarjei Vesaas or Johan Falkberget. Agnar and Knut would also read aloud to each other whenever they were together. It was Agnar who first introduced Knut to Olav H. Hauge's poetry. In autumn of that year, Olav had been awarded the Norwegian Critics Prize for *På Ørnetuva*. The publication gave rise to heated debate since he had broken expectations about what a poem's correct form and content should be. His poetry was new and different. His technique deconstructed the strict stanzas, with their clear rhymes and rhythms, of standard Norwegian poetry and revolved around small things close to his heart: an apple tree, an axe, a cat, and even the farmer's cooperative that didn't want any more bottle-shaped apples in the poem "I chopped down the tall apple tree outside my window." Olav's poetry struck a powerful chord with Agnar and Knut, which is why it felt completely natural for them to head to Voss to purchase a copy of *På Ørnetuva*.

"Unfortunately, Agnar wasn't destined to live long. He was a sharp boy, far above average, and performed extremely well at school. He had a particular talent for theory, and with his fantastic, adhesive memory he could remember everything. At the young age of 26, he drowned himself in the fjord outside his house, after having suffered from mental illness his whole life. He simply couldn't take it anymore. It was a great friendship for as long as it lasted."

In 1964, Knut attended and played at one of the many gatherings put on by the Hardanger Spelemannslag (Hardanger Folk Music Association) in Granvin's cultural center. Geirr Tveitt at the piano accompanied the dance, and Olav H. Hauge gave a reading. This was the first time Knut met his master-to-be. Yet their first proper meeting would not come until somewhere around 1972, when they began to hold occasional joint performances of music and poetry.

In 1977, Knut had begun teaching Hardanger fiddle classes in Ulvik, a mere stone's throw from where Olav spent his days picking apples and writing poetry. Before long, they were sharing dialogues in Olav's home. Dialogues that would last over twenty years. From then until Olav's dying day, Knut visited his friend and teacher in his Ulvik home once or twice a week. All year, every year.

MONOLOGUES AT ROSSVOLL

Olav H. Hauge's house had no calendar of any kind to keep track of their appointments. Knut just popped in when he felt like it, and was always welcome. If too much time had passed between visits, then Olav would ring him up and ask him to come over. Knut had read a wide selection of books before beginning these regular visits to Olav's house, but the Folkedal Public Library didn't have much by poets like Li Po when he was growing up. So a lot of what Olav talked about was completely new for Knut.

"I felt a great need to check out every single book he mentioned from the library, a wealth of poets and philosophers. After a while, he came to expect this from me, and at a rather fast pace. Sometimes I wouldn't get the time to read up on everything I had meant to by our next session. Then he would come out with something along the lines of, 'Hell, haven't you read that yet?' He found it unbelievable that I could take so much time. Was there anything more important?"

You name Olav H. Hauge as one of your most pivotal teachers. But what do you make of the fact that he wasn't a musician?

"Our master-student relationship consisted of endless discussions and debates on countless topics, such as art, religion, writing, music, philosophy, politics, and history. In a way, my sessions with Olav were like going to university. But instead of entering the university in Bergen, my classroom was a living room in Rossvoll. And instead of limiting lectures to 45 minutes at a time, we could go on for hours, all day long. I listened while Olav served up long monologues, pacing around the room, swearing, shouting, and flailing his arms as his excitement grew. Questions gushed out of me and answers washed in. Really, we were doing the same thing, working toward an optimal form of self-expression. That was how we found a common language, despite the fact that our art forms were different. For me, these monologues were just as crucial and character-building as any of my innumerable fiddling sessions. A broad general education is essential. Everything eventually makes its way into the music."

This all sounds like an apprenticeship in becoming human?

"That's right. I took Olav's ethos to heart: To always be respectful, to try to tone down your own taste, to reject nothing, to attempt everything with equal enthusiasm, and to always speak courteously about others. He had a big heart, and had nothing but encouragement and constructive feedback for new poets. I was also lucky enough to run into other notable persons at his house, including Espen Skjønberg, Robert Bly, and several of the radical 1960s poets like Jan Erik Vold, Tor Obrestad, and others."

Olav H. Hauge and Knut Hamre on the poet's garden bench in Rossvoll, Ulvik in 1980.

Olav advised Knut to never lose hold of his curiosity, to read and to philosophize, and for that reason recommended writers like Søren Kierkegaard, who he thought to be a crucial spiritual infusion for any artist. The same went for Friedrich Nietzsche, who claimed that life revolves around always working hard and avoiding easy solutions.

"Olav defended the value of wisdom and hard work, too. He didn't believe that people should just sit around and wait for inspiration to arrive. We also had many debates about philosophy in general. He lectured me in depth on a broad range of authors, about whether he liked them or not, and at these points I would raise a question like: Why do you think Knut Hamsun wrote the way he did? Or: What do you think about Henrik Ibsen's poetry? I don't actually recall him ever not knowing about something I quizzed him on. Not once."

On the temple bell

Sleeps

A butterfly

Yosa Buson

Through his lectures at Olav's home, Knut learned about a grander point of view: That nothing is separate from anything else and that everything is interconnected in a vast universe. From the microscopic to the galactic, from the tiniest seed to the mightiest star—just like Buson's butterfly on the enormous temple bell. And they would discuss the relationship between nature and art, between humanity and the universe at large. They realized that nothing stands alone in a little box, but always becomes waves that ripple into anything and everything else.

"I recognize that same philosophy in everything he wrote— that the local and the global are one."

Now and then Knut would play for Olav, to ask for his advice. Olav would mostly respond by commenting on the colors of each piece. For example, if Knut played the *huldreslått*[8] "Bygdatråen," then Olav would talk about dark shades he saw in it, and suggest that Knut pronounce them more deeply.

"He could also be quite critical, and would always say outright if he felt like I was holding myself back during certain refrains. Naturally, since he couldn't play music himself, he would listen to my music in a different way, and it was wise to ask advice from ears like those. If he did ever mention music itself, then it was usually just a coincidence."

In the 1980s, Olav began criticizing Knut for competing so often at *kappleikar*. He thought it was the worst way for Knut to use his music, to compete to see who was "the best." Yet he was also always the first one to brag about Knut to others about how many trophies Knut had back at home. There was little consistency to his criticism. You didn't get sent home with any fast words of wisdom. Olav's opinions would change every time Knut met with him.

"It was the same with his writing. If people came up to Olav and asked him outright about what he made of a sentence, an interpretation or so on, then he would turn them away. You have to think for yourself. The unspoken has a great power; you really make a great mess of things if you try and explain them all."

Did you learn much about stage technique from Olav when you held concerts together?

"His stage presence made a deep impression. His message and the way he got it across were astounding. Olav convinced you to listen. I never saw him looking frightened on stage, only beforehand. He would get anxious long before he ever arrived at the venue, and this developed to such a mad extent toward the end of his career that he began to cancel the trips themselves. He got sour and moody when all the conflicts inside him began to clash. His explanations for why he couldn't make it were always numerous, and sometimes rather funny, too. He once rang me mere seconds before I left to pick him up in Ulvik and drive him to a concert in Bergen. He sadly wouldn't be able to make it because his little cat had gone missing and he had to stay at home in case it came back. Yet as soon as he stepped onto the stage, all of this washed away, and he had full control."

It sounds like he might actually have enjoyed the limelight, as long as he managed to set aside all the doubt leading up to it?

"He would always naturally become the center of attention, something that he enjoyed tremendously. Now and then to such a degree that I almost couldn't get him to come home again."

FROM APPLE SPRAYING TO THE QURAN

Olav H. Hauge was always a champion of the underdog. He held a great sympathy for all those who had fallen off the wagon, or for those who formed a threat to the status quo. He would tell similar stories about himself, as a square-peg boy growing up in a small rural community. Olav was the oddball who could never stop himself reading books and poetry. He also took frequent trips in and out of psychiatric hospitals when he was younger.

"I remember Olav describing both his multiple mental ailments and the time he spent at mental hospitals as positive experiences, especially for his poetry. He had seen and experienced things in his own mind that went beyond people's normal boundaries and limitations. There, he was free to sit still for a whole day just staring at clouds. When common sense and theory went out the window, all forms of self-expression grew stronger. He showed me that even if life threw the worst challenges at you, it was still possible to get by. That really made an impression on me."

Olav H. Hauge was proud and wise, and would quickly get bored with the people he met if they didn't have any chemistry. This could make him lose his temper, and burst out with brash truisms, like: "*Nynorsk* is earth and *Bokmål* is air!"[9] Hauge generally had an attitude that was extraordinarily caring and inclusive, but enjoyed it tremendously when he got to take people down a few notches. Especially those with higher education. He would exclaim: "I've never been to any kind of university, but bloody hell, surely an academic like you must be well aware of this!"

Yet all humans were equal in his eyes. He had a great gift for accepting different peoples and their interest. Which was why he would resolve most social situations by diving into discussions on anything from ditch digging and apple tree spraying to the Quran.

What do you make of all the myths that surrounded Olav H. Hauge?

"The image many people have of Olav as a quiet and shy man are probably only partly true. Olav's life, first and foremost, was a life of reading. If I paid him a visit, he might not have had a single visitor since the last time I came. In the meantime, his head had been swelling up with ideas and thoughts, blowing up into a gigantic bubble that was ready to burst the moment I stepped onto his apple farm. Olav probably spent a lot of his life alone. Yet once he got talking, he could chatter a hole into the head of anyone who was ready to listen. I remember once being on a car journey with him. His wife, Bodil Cappelen, was driving, I was sitting next to her and Olav was in the backseat. He soon grew bored of sitting back there all alone, and this towering, energetic man ended up sticking his head and torso between the front seats, brandishing his arms around and delivering lectures that went on forever. Thank heavens he was so eager to share his thoughts! Otherwise, we would have missed out on so much of his knowledge."

Did you have to pay at all for any of these monologues?

"No, but now and then I did like to help him with practical jobs, like laying bricks and so on, since I was an educated bricklayer."

Didn't you have an employer wondering where you were, then, when you often spent a whole day at Olav's house?

"Do you know, I've never thought about that. Being there was basically a job in itself!"

What does Olav mean to you?

"He gave me comfort, and was a true friend I could always depend on. His home was a safe space, where you really had time to dig into what was important. It all felt so normal and nice. No drama. We brewed coffee, fried bacon, and, when we couldn't bring ourselves to jabber away any more, we would shoot cans of fishcakes with his bow and arrow. I remember him always saying: 'Keep on doing what you do, Knut, keep to what's yours.' When all the opposition to my music became too much for me, this advice gave me the strength to carry on. In those vulnerable moments, his words were like a life raft."

Was the feeling mutual?

"I know I helped Olav. He would often bring me along to events I wasn't invited to, like when he was going to some kind of festive gathering, for example, and was worried it might all get a bit dull. Or when he attended prize ceremonies, and so on."

What was it like to be left behind when such a prominent master and friend died?

"Fortunately, Olav was an old man. He didn't go in a hurry. I had plenty of time with him."

HOLDING ON
TO RUNNING WATER

The folk music community in Norway fixates on handing down its musical tradition as faithfully to the original as possible. Yet in truth the tradition changes constantly, depending on the popular aesthetic trends of each new period's fiddlers and teachers. One of the reasons for this is that folk music is mostly based on an oral tradition, instead of formal musical notation. Even today, despite how recording equipment has been available for decades, and more folk musicians than ever are able to read music, the discipline is mostly passed between fiddlers in person, from ear to ear.

It's a vulnerable genre, which means much of it has already been lost to time. Perhaps because the music wasn't right for the period, or there weren't enough disciples around to inherit the knowledge. But can a deep respect for our musical heritage and a sense of humility get the upper hand and manage to stop the river from flowing freely? What about villspelet (wild play), the improvisations that Torgeir Augundsson ("Myllarguten") was supposed to have played during his best performances? Are today's bearers of tradition as free as he was said to have been? Or have we, for fear of losing parts of our tradition, ended up losing this side of our playing already? Perhaps parts of the past deserve to be lost?

Within the inner circles of the Norwegian folk music community, there are constant debates over whether there is too much or too little preservation and renewal of our traditions. Knut believes that this controversy provides enough friction to create a much-needed impetus. Because without forward movement, folk music will surely die. At the same time, however, if the pressure to hold on to tradition becomes too intense, then our music will definitely begin to stagnate. Knut feels that it is essential that musicians feel free from this pressure, but he has also known certain folk musicians, when encouraged to make use of this freedom, tend toward complacency. This is because the anxiety of influences from the past and our attempts to avoid making references might sometimes get out of hand. The main problem is finding a way to create and interpret folk music freely and instinctively, without imposing too many set rules. Some people might not want to be forced into this literate musical past, but such a desire for freedom can sometimes become a constraint in and of itself. Unfortunately, it is all too easy for a liberated, improvising fiddle player to feel mentally stifled by the more conservative fiddlers, who would rather have everything played by the book, and those who want everything but.

"I have often experienced other people's doubts about what I have done, and am doing, to the tradition in terms of style. All these naysayers used to get on my nerves, but now I realize that I need them. They force me to be more aware of what I want and don't want to do as a musician. Personally, I draw a clear line in my head between teaching and being a performing musician. For me, they are two completely distinct roles. As Knut the musician, I feel free to play and express myself however I want to. I think about other things when I'm playing, and inserting improvisations here and there in the moment has always been a natural, liberating part of my renditions. As a teacher, on the other hand, I would much rather pass down tradition as faithfully and precisely as possible, as I first learned it myself. Regardless of what most people think, it's not our collective history or our artistic influences that restrict our musical freedom but ourselves, through our constant attempts to control and manage one another."

Knut has a theory that the fiddle players in and around Granvin used to be far more open-minded before his time. He uses as an

Knut Hamre playing at a live NRK radio broadcast at "Gamle Logen" in Oslo 1990.

example the fiddle maker Håvard Kvandal's story about Olav Håstabø's wedding in 1881, when he and fiddler Hans Selland played together for the guests. The crowd had been impressed by how they performed the same tune at the same time, in total unison. This was unheard of back then, which suggests that most of the guests were accustomed to fiddlers always playing a tune with their own individual variations. They weren't always so uptight about how each tune should be played, or where it came from, so long as the music was good. Many fiddlers after 1910, when the gramophone arrived, learned classical pieces, as well as tunes of all sorts from travelers passing through the area.

"Anders Kjerland was once listening to a piece of music on BBC radio, when he suddenly exclaimed: 'But that's Nils Tjoflot's tune!' The penny had just dropped for Anders: A fiddler from the neighboring village had probably learned this piece of music from cruise ship tourists on their way to Utne and Granvin in the late 1800s. And yet, here was Anders, thinking it was Tjoflot's own composition the whole time."

As Knut sees it, the way many folk musicians today worry over preserving tradition is nothing new. Folk music has always been under such pressure. The fiddler Knut Dahle from Tinn, for example, was already writing letters in the 1880s to Edvard Grieg in hopes that the famous composer might like to transcribe the fiddle tunes Dahle knew. He was extremely troubled by the idea that the fiddle music would disappear with him. Johan Halvorsen wrote down the tunes on Grieg's behalf, and Grieg subsequently used and rearranged many of them for the piano in such works as his *Norwegian Peasant Dances*, Op. 72.

Perhaps the way people are so willing to fight to preserve their musical heritage is due to their own personal desire to cling to something they already know and are therefore comforted by?

"You're right. But I worry that people have based their understanding of how the old tunes of Hardanger 'used to sound' more on nostalgia than actual knowledge. It isn't possible to know, since there are only a few fragments of evidence about how a small number of fiddlers might have played their instruments before 1900, and there are no recordings before 1903."

Many traditional fiddlers and singers, myself included, are disappointed when they realize that being a great traditional musician will never be enough. It turns out that in order to be exciting and new to our audiences, journalists, and concert organizers, the cards have decreed that we should also be "cutting-edge." On the other hand, you hear about people feeling suffocated by the claustrophobic pressure of having to faithfully preserve their heritage. Surely there must be room for both points of view?

"We certainly do need both. The free spirits and the traditionalists. I am convinced that all of this uproar stems from how much the wants of other people influence our own actions, and the extent we are willing to change ourselves in order to suit these fickle desires and ideals. *That* is what truly restricts our musical freedom, not old archived recordings! Although, when I think about it, it does seem strange that we stick labels like 'cutting-edge' or 'traditional' on people at all. Almost as if there were some direct conflict and friction between being so-called traditionalists and innovators. At the end of the day, aren't we all just fiddle players?"

Some would claim that recordings of our folk music have been both a blessing and a curse, as they may have led to the subsequent standardization of fiddle tunes. Old recordings, such as Ola Mosafinn's from 1912, soon became the precedent for how a tune should be played. When certain people listen to these recordings, they might think, "So this was how Ola Mosafinn played." But by the time these recordings were made, Mosafinn was already an old man. How Mosafinn played when he was twenty, or even fifty years old, we may only guess. But probably not in the same way he was playing in 1912.

"Some people find comfort in these old sources, some do not. But if we all end up becoming a gang of copycats, then our art will slowly but surely die out. I'm certain of that. In all honesty, I think it's good for some of our heritage to fade away. Although it would naturally become a problem if it all did. Yet now that recordings exist, I hope we can turn our energies toward more important things than just trying to commemorate everything. We no longer need to be afraid, like Knut Dahle was. Over the past eighty-odd years, we have managed to document a huge treasure trove of music."

I've heard you say that the best way to preserve our tradition is by allowing music to thrive in the hands of the fiddler, and not just in dusty old archives. Some people believe that the best music will always survive. But this is a naïve way of thinking. There have been a great many excellent fiddle tunes that have almost disappeared from our repertoire, just because they differed from the ruling fashions of their era.

"Recordings or no, the most important thing is that today, lots of people have been taught a good grasp of the craft itself, so they can validate the old tunes, at least in terms of the actual music. That counts for a lot more than someone being able to recite every single one of Hardanger's 500 to 600 fiddle tunes by heart."

TONALITY, GROUP PLAYING, AND COMPOSING IN THE MOMENT

The Hardanger fiddle started being played alongside other instruments besides military drums just over a century ago. Compared with other folk music traditions, this is not a particularly long time. It caused quite a sensation in the 1920s when Anders Kjerland played at dances in Granvin to the accompaniment of a pump organ. People would come simply to watch. The pump organ is tuned in equal temperament, which means it cannot be used to play microtones. There is an abundance of microtonality in Norwegian folk music. Since Anders Kjerland's performances, joint collaborations with equally tempered instruments like the organ, accordion, and fretted guitar have increased substantially within Norwegian folk music, especially during the past two or three decades. Many people believe this has pushed Hardanger fiddle music into an ongoing process of tonal standardization.

"We need to remain aware of this, now more than ever. What kind of compromises must we make with our own music when we play it with equal-tempered instruments? What do we gain? What do we lose? Is it running against of the fundamental aesthetics of our music? I don't want to be a stick in the mud, and realistically speaking, a lot of this comes down to taste. Some individuals could well feel that the music has been standardized, both in terms of melody and rhythm. The dominant folk music on Norwegian radio and at festivals has begun sounding just like the genres you hear all the time, like pop music and folk songs, not to mention American country music. Yet I am still not one of these people who insist on the Hardanger fiddle being a solo instrument and nothing else. I've tried every kind of collaboration, some that worked and others that didn't. But if you want this craft to survive and go beyond its home region, you need to hold on to what's unique about it.

I would guess that if we watered down our peculiarities, we would be destroying our own future as folk musicians, too."

Perhaps the amount of change happening within traditional folk music in Hardanger and abroad is simply the price we have to pay for choosing to open ourselves to all these new cultural movements.

"Maybe you need to be ready to lose something in order to gain something. Striking the perfect balance between being open or closed to cultural influences is crucial. The first sign of the impending extinction of an art form is when its artists are no longer willing to accept anything from the wider world outside of their small, geographically restricted location. We need both the local and the global, the big ideas and the small. All of it inside us, at the same time. In everything."

Anders Kjerland and his cousin Sigurd Kjerland (playing pump organ) .
Photo taken around 1927.

The music of the Hardanger fiddle has almost always been composed for, and played as, solo performances. Much of the instrument's traditional *slåttemusikk* consists of deeply intricate compositions, which many people claim sound best when played alone. This means that making new arrangements based on these tunes can sometimes be a complicated process. It is hard to adapt these tunes by borrowing from other genres, since Hardanger fiddle music isn't based on standard chords or organized in regular structures like the AABA format, as you find in popular music, standards, or *gamaldans* (old-time dance tunes). Instead, the themes in traditional *slåttemusikk* flow almost imperceptibly from one into another. Each of these themes contains a set of short motifs that are sewn together into musical phrases. These melodic phrases, which are of varying length, determine the structure of the tune. In addition, *slåttemusikk* cannot always be defined by a set time signature. Neither fiddler nor dancers think about the actual beats of the rhythm, because every fiddle tune has its own ceaseless pulse that keeps beating away no matter what. And if one asks a traditional fiddle player to indicate a downbeat, most will not be able to give you a straight answer, since they have never thought about it in those terms.

I know these strange shifts in rhythm can be bewildering for listeners and accompanists of Hardanger fiddle music, which is probably one of the reasons why so many people consider it to be inaccessible. I have even seen musicians who are dazzlingly talented at their own complicated forms of music shake their head and give up the second they hear it. And sometimes a bit too soon, sadly.

"Sometimes people feel overwhelmed when they are confronted with Hardanger fiddle music, like they have nothing to contribute. It already has everything it 'needs,' in some shape or form. And that I can understand. All music has its own code you need to learn to crack. *Slåttemusikk* is no exception. But maybe it just requires a little more time to do so, since most people have never heard this sort of music before."

Most Norwegian folk musicians change their playing somewhat, too, but I think only a select few really take it beyond the confines of the tradition. Two who did this are Bjarne Herrefoss and Eivind Mo.

"Bjarne had the gift of being able to capture a moment, as did Eivind. There is a constant restlessness in Eivind's recordings, always moving forward, and rarely, if ever, repeating the same motif. I spent a lot of time in the 1970s visiting Eivind to learn tunes from him. Back then, he could occasionally conjure up fully-fledged pieces of *slåttemusikk* through improvisation. If I hadn't had a tape recorder on hand in those moments, then gems like 'Steinars Minne' would probably have disappeared the moment Eivind played his last note."

Surely the fact that Hardanger fiddle music isn't based on chords means you can't really improvise with it in the same way you can with jazz, rock, or blues music, when you have a chord scheme to guide you. One can use the modes it's based on, of course, but there isn't any explicit spoken or written practice in this regard.

"Correct. That's why we have to think a little differently to be able to conjure up poetic melodies in the moment, while making new variations in a tune's themes, double stops, sounds, and ornamentations. It is also common practice for us fiddlers to improvise around the same rhythmic patterns, but we rarely break with the pulse of a fiddle tune."

But are there no instructions or "fiddling rules" about how you should do this?

"No, we have very few established strategies. When we need to improvise today, our minds tend to quickly turn to jazz or likeminded music, which can get in the way. My first port of call when it comes to getting tips and inspiration for improvisation is listening to and taking notes from Eivind Mo and Halldor Meland. In all honesty, I've worked with improvisation for such a long time now that I probably have developed a sort of path or a way to do it, yet I can't really say precisely what it is. But it's there. The freedom that allows my music to flow out of me naturally has only ever come to me after playing a lot over a long period of time. If nothing else, we can be sure that improvisation is not a result of being lazy."

I have heard many musicians claim that the best improvisations are those that are already composed. These improvisations are like ready sketches—complete, alternative compositions that you can choose to bring out whenever you feel like it.

"Yes, that is certainly one approach. I feel that improvisation needs to add something to a fiddle tune. The fiddler Kjetil Løndal used to play a tune once through exactly as he had heard it, then play more freely and improvise with it during his second rendition. Eivind Mo claimed the point of improvising was to put the original on display. And in all art forms, there are a number of unwritten rules. We can try to be open-minded or stubborn, but the classics of the Hardanger fiddle tradition have been experimented with so many times that it is often the music itself which decides whether a variation sounds good. A wise and observant fiddler follows its guiding hand."

But isn't it important to take chances when you improvise?

"Oh, absolutely. The musician can't paint over their music if they didn't like the sound, for it disappears the moment it is played. But there is a peculiarly liberating feeling when you surrender yourself to the ephemeral nature of music. It is here, and then it is gone."

MASTER
AND STUDENT

Knut has contributed a great deal to the teaching of the Hardanger fiddle in its native region. Not only has he had copious amounts of students over almost four decades, but many of his students are now considered to be among the best folk musicians in all of Norway. Artists and musicians from countless genres and different artistic backgrounds are constantly coming from far and wide to learn from this generous, patient teacher. Many have also visited Knut in order to study his pedagogical methods and find out exactly what is going on in Hardanger.

2012 | Early one morning, I decide to give Knut a call. I have been practicing with my Hardanger fiddle for a long time, perhaps too long, and I can't get anywhere with it. I haven't felt like this only today, but for quite a while.

"It feels strange," I tell him. "I have played so much over the past few years, faced many challenges, and taken part in many concerts, recordings, and the like over a relatively short period of time. But deep down, it still feels like I haven't taken a single step forward. In fact, the older I get, the *less* I feel I can do. And the more validation I receive, the more anxiety I feel. Even though I'm 29 years old and have played ever since I was eight, it feels as though I'm still a beginner."

"That's how I feel, too. Like I've only just begun."

"But you're over sixty!"

"Yes, but I still feel the same way. I always try to keep myself in this beginner phase. One must never forget to view the world, its peoples, and an old fiddle tune with fresh eyes, like those of a child. As Pablo Picasso once said: 'It took me a year to learn to paint like Raphael, but it took me a lifetime to be able to paint like a child.' In other words, the goal is never to feel finished with learning. If you still feel like you're an absolute beginner, then you should be grateful. For in many ways, your journey as an artist really *has* only just begun. It is only when you have fully mastered the craft itself and have a grasp of all its theory that your life and deep spiritual journey truly begin. Maybe you should take a break from practicing for a bit and instead work on opening up your mind, so that you enter into a constant state of motion and flow."

Our conversation comes to an end and I hang up the phone. As I do so, I muse over how fantastic it is that we agree on teaching as a never-ending process. It doesn't revolve around twenty-two-minute lessons and exams, but dedicating a lifetime to learning a subject as thoroughly as possible, then passing it on. I put my fiddle back into its case. As Knut was hinting, I have probably practiced more than long enough. As he always says: "We have to remember that we are in service of music and music is not in service of us." I look through my window and gaze outside at the budding sprigs. I try to feel at peace, yet also in motion, as I open my child's eyes.

1974 | Knut Hamre is walking to a rehearsal in Granvin's youth center, which has been arranged by the Hardanger Folk Music Association. When he opens the door, he is hit by a gust of damp air. Inside, the culture center is throbbing with young, new faces as the sounds of several dozen Hardanger fiddles ring out. Knut, along with the more experienced members of the association, are overwhelmed. Where did all these people wanting to learn the fiddle spring from all of a sudden? None of them can remember there ever being such a large gathering before.

Fiddlers of all ages open up their cases to reveal fiddles new and old. A few fiddlers start rosining their bows, while others are bowing and plucking their fiddles, drinking coffee, and chatting with one another. Knut is their instructor today and bellows through the din, telling the crowd to pay attention, because practice is about to begin. The tune they are learning today is "Rull as played by Severin Kjerland". The room falls silent and everyone turns their eyes and ears toward Knut, who starts off by playing the entire tune once through. He then divides it up, playing the first section over and over, to make it easier for people to remember the melody. Everyone raises their bows, from the very youngest of students to those with fifty years of experience, and the hum of fiddles starts up once more as they all try to imitate Knut as well as they can.

THE BEGINNING

"What makes a master a good master? It is when a master takes joy in his student becoming better than himself. Then the master might learn something from his student."

Odd Nerdrum

It pleases Knut no end that so many people are willing to come and learn the music he holds so dear. The same music that, when he was a boy, next to no one wanted to learn. But gradually he notices that all these fresh beginners, who are so dearly welcome and wanted, simply can't keep up. There isn't enough time or space to work on technique during these group lessons at the Hardanger Folk Music Association, and many of the younger learners will never move forward without one-on-one instruction. Knut thinks that something needs to change in order to support a new generation of fiddle players in the Hardanger region.

Some years later in 1980, he applies for a grant from Hordaland County to start providing Hardanger fiddle lessons for locals in the region. Knut begins doing so in Ulvik later that year. He hires a classroom in the town's horticultural school and hosts sessions there between the vegetable patches, teaching *springar* and *rull* to students young and old. While Knut is providing free lectures on the Hardanger fiddle in Ulvik, other forms of musical education in Norway are slowly moving from the private sector into the hands of municipal authorities. Schools specializing in music tuition are established, and slowly spread across the country. Nowadays this type of school is called a *kulturskule*, or "culture school."[10] The idea of a music school reaches Hardanger in 1984, and in 1985 a position opens up for a Hardanger fiddle teacher across the parishes of Granvin, Ulvik, Eidfjord, and Ullensvang. Thus, Hardanger becomes the first region to offer students the chance to learn the Hardanger fiddle at its music schools.

Knut gets the job as the music school's Hardanger fiddle teacher. Every week he sets off from his home in Granvin's Folkedal, driving first to Øvre Eidfjord to visit a few students there, and so on to Nedre Eidfjord. He stops to visit a student in Bu before driving on to Kinsarvik, Opedal, and Sekse in the parish of Ullensvang. As day shifts into night, Knut takes the ferry back across the fjord and drives home. The next day, the parish of Ulvik is on the itinerary and Granvin the day after that. And so it carries on. Week after week, year after year. The days and lessons are many and long, and the numbers of Knut's students and miles traveled continue to grow.

"When I first started out at the music school, I remember the head teacher telling me, 'If you still have that job in five years, then you're a darn good teacher!' No one thought so many people would want to learn the Hardanger fiddle, and no one thought I would enjoy the amount of traveling required of me to teach my students. But I've held my position continuously for more than thirty years, although with a fluctuating amount of employment."

Today there are around 80 students playing the Hardanger fiddle through the various culture schools of Hardanger. Knut has typically had at least 60 students during any given semester of his teaching career. Around 30 of those students are in Ullensvang parish alone. In the parish's culture school, more students have chosen to learn the Hardanger fiddle than any other instrument.

"This is rather strange, given how the Hardanger fiddle is completely outside of today's familiar youth culture, far away from the kind of music young people usually listen to. It's difficult to fathom why so many students still want to play the fiddle, but it's fortunate things have turned out this way."

MORE PLAY THAN WORK

Yet it wasn't all bouquets and applause for Knut when he started teaching at the music school.

Skepticism over the decision came from two factions. One was worried that it would cause the Hardanger Folk Music Association to lose its role as an educational body. This was a valid concern. The other was more worried about the notion of everyone learning to "play just like Knut Hamre." Knut felt that in any case, *that* was unlikely to happen, and turned the question back around on those who doubted him: What was the alternative? Did they want people to learn the fiddle or not? The person most involved in all of Knut's pedagogical work was Sigbjørn Bernhoft Osa (1910-1990). He was particularly open-minded, and would show up unannounced at lessons and group sessions to give advice. He was an inspiration to Knut and everyone else he came into contact with. Sigbjørn was a playful soul, saying things to his younger pupils like: "Yes, yes, now we all gobble up our fiddles!" He would then make scraping sounds with his hands under the table while pretending to gnaw on his fiddle.

"He was simply the best with children. His sheer presence made me feel good by the fact that someone was watching over me. An early comfort in a profession I had little experience in."

In the early 1980s, Knut took a course in the renowned Suzuki Method, named after Japanese violinist Shinichi Suzuki (1898-1998). The method revolves around the idea that all children are born with the natural skills to learn a language and that, like learning a language, they can learn music by attempting to emulate what they see and hear. Yet no matter what age you are, this method will still help you master a skill. The Suzuki Method also emphasizes group learning, where students are encouraged to engage in playfulness rather than forced expertise.

"This theory was almost groundbreaking for me. I had never heard anyone say it was okay to play your way to mastery before. It was completely at odds with Germany's and the earlier Soviet Union's strict schools of thought, which in simplest terms revolved around learning the techniques and practicing scales."

The course provided Knut with many new ideas, with particular regard to collaborative learning, which involved learning short melodies in groups, holding small concerts for one another, and playing together. Knut took those aspects of the Suzuki Method that seemed natural to him and welded them to his own theories and experiences to form his own pedagogical technique. Knut never truly departed from the idea of one-on-one teaching. Anything else would have been inconceivable.

"For some people, the social aspect is the best thing about these sessions. But there will always be a loner who has to do everything on their own, in their special way. These types always need one-on-one lessons to really blossom. There are certainly benefits to doing things together, especially with beginners, but eventually comes the need to do things with each individual student. And an individual's needs have nothing to do with age."

What else has inspired what I and your other students like to call the "Knut Method"?

"My own teachers, of course. But a combination of trial and error and life experiences have paved the way more than anything else. There weren't any educators on hand at the culture school who could instruct me on how to teach this instrument. I was alone on this one. But I found inspiration by reading about the pedagogical approaches of violinists Yehudi Menuhin and Jascha Heifetz, among others, and I also took courses with Sigbjørn Bernhoft Osa."

THE KNUT METHOD'S FOUR PHASES

A young student comes hurrying into the classroom where Knut is teaching, carrying a worn-out fiddle case in one hand.

Many hands have owned this case before him, but today is his first-ever fiddle lesson. Knut opens up his new student's case and tells him that this instrument needs to become a part of his body, and that he should be proud of it, not afraid of it. They start by learning how to hold the fiddle, and Knut checks whether this new student's scrawny frame suits the instrument in the first place. Next they figure out the right way to hold it against his neck, and stretch out his left hand as far as it will go so that his fingertips can reach the fingerboard. Then it is time for the bow. It always takes a little longer to get the hang of the bow, but Knut tells the child that he needs to imagine he is holding something he cares for, something nice, and the young student's nervous fingers begin to loosen. They carefully run the bow along each string, one at a time. It creaks a little, but Knut reassures the student and plays a little melody himself. Then he starts teaching the tune, little by little. He does so slowly and carefully, because Knut would much rather the child feel confident and get the hang of the instrument than progress quickly. The new student realizes that there aren't any understrings on his fiddle and feels disappointed. Isn't a Hardanger fiddle supposed to have them? Knut explains it is easier to start off learning with just the four strings. That way he can look forward to getting some more! Knut makes a recording of the tune, so the student has something to refer to when practicing at home. Knut never writes anything down. He wants his new student to develop the ability to memorize melodies as soon as possible.

This might go on for years, before they eventually move on to the second phase of the student's education. Then Knut will start giving his student recordings of his other students and colleagues, and asking them to listen to particular fiddle tunes. This is also when Knut starts giving explanations about the history of the fiddle and its players.

"It goes without saying that if you want to learn an art form, you need to know what it's all about, and listening to it logically helps you crack the music's code. If you learn to love a type of music, then you will learn it faster and better. When I started out teaching, I thought that the history and music of the fiddle was common knowledge to most students. But I realized that now there is a whole lot more that needs to be included in these fiddle sessions. Today, most students at the beginning of their musical education with me have no previous connection to folk music. There is less casual, amateurish fiddle playing going on, and the social norms around it have changed. This means you don't automatically get exposed to this music before stepping inside the door of the culture school. When you're a teacher nowadays, you have to come to terms with this reality and accept the consequences."

In his third phase, Knut instructs his student in greater detail with regard to the craft itself: about various fiddle tunes, styles, rhythms and techniques. He teaches them about how fiddle styles vary depending on where in Hardanger each piece of music comes from, and which past fiddle players have influenced each style. The student tends to mature mentally and emotionally during this phase, as debates about personal expression start coming to the fore. Knut listens intently while his student plays, commenting and posing problems as they arise. For this reason, the third phase is pivotal for correction, as this is usually the point when the student is willing to take everything in without much resistance. For this reason, the master needs to remain aware that anything he says during this phase can often have a great effect on a student.

After fifteen to twenty years of this, depending on the student, Knut will move into his fourth and final phase. At this point, everything flows. Knut just sits there listening, and students come and go as they please. In this phase, Knut is more vague and less precise, and his role as teacher becomes less clear. Debates around aesthetics begin to dominate the session, as the student's artistry slowly emerges. Knut still tries to stay away from any formal analysis, and to minimize any systematic or theoretical approaches to music. Instead, he tries to open up the student's heart to what feels intuitive.

"There isn't any template you have to blindly follow with everyone. As their master, you have to be wise and attentive, trust your instincts, and pay attention to when the time is right to move into the next phase. But if the student lacks either the talent, self-discipline, or desire to learn the discipline, then it doesn't matter how talented the master is. There has to be two-way communication in the relationship if it's going to work. You need to be speaking the same language. It demands a lot from both the student and their master."

Another pedagogical technique Knut uses is inviting his students to collaborate with him on various projects, such as CD recordings and concerts. Many of his past students have done so, and he still offers the opportunity to his new, talented students today. Knut believes in the importance of having shared experiences. It also helps his students feel comfortable entering into new situations. Knut has occasionally even invited his eldest students to substitute for him as teacher.

"I have made a few bold choices. But as far as I know, they have usually worked out."

When I was younger, it felt like such an honor to be asked to collaborate on projects with you. At the same time, I felt like it was a kind of stamp of approval from you, to say that we were equals. Even though you were the master and I was the student. It comforted me immensely.

"In my opinion, that feeling of equality is the very essence of success toward calling out the best in your students."

I know that, after a while, you tend to encourage your students to seek out other teachers. You even did so to me, which I wasn't particularly happy about. But I presume there was a plan behind this, too?

"Remember that none of my students is ever forced to leave me, but it is important for all of them to gain a wider perspective of the Hardanger fiddle's heritage. To try and find out about the variety of styles across a geographic area, about the different bearers of the tradition, the different techniques used, the fiddle's history, and so on. You weren't the only one of my students to react in the way you did when I suggested this, but you must never allow art and music to fall into routine. The same goes for me. It is important to take a hiatus now and then."

But sometimes breaks can lead to conflict, especially when the student encounters a new master who is harder to communicate with.

"In that case, you just need to cut ties and walk away. This is the good thing about these master-student relationships: You aren't locked into a system where you have to stick with the same master, or the same student, year after year. If a relationship between a master and a student is to last for a long time, then you *need* good chemistry. If you don't have that, then it will be a waste of time and resources for both parties."

But surely it is no easy feat for a young student to come out and say, "I don't think this is working. I want to find myself a new teacher"?

"I think it is the responsibility of the master, not the student, to break off a mentorship that isn't working."

What makes a good master?

"When he appreciates his student doing well. A master needs to have unconditional love and generosity in their heart, and be able to view each individual pupil for who they truly are, and support them in that. If not, then the master will end up holding their student back. Fear ruins most teaching relationships. A good teacher should also be able to spark an unstoppable force in their student, a kind of burning motivation that helps them carry on doing what they want to do, and be ready to learn everything there is to learn. Finally, the term 'master' implies that you need to have mastered something. In order to teach someone, you obviously need to know your art."

You say that feeling secure is important for calling out the best in your students. But aren't there also cases where a large amount of pressure from a teacher can bring out good things in their students, too?

"Pressure works with certain personalities—for a while. But I doubt you could ever inspire a true love of music that way. And if a student doesn't have that, they don't have very much after all. Giving someone a push is good, and sometimes needed. But I don't believe in using pressure."

Of course, not all master-student relationships work equally well.

"No, but I'm still sure that when they *do* work, they are definitely the best form of teaching. They provide a unique space for students to express their individuality and independence, and that is *exactly* what our art needs. Maybe there aren't many master-student relationships that last lifetimes. If they are to survive, the egos of both student and master need to be kept in balance. Otherwise, they fall apart. These relationships revolve around trust, respect, and equality between masters and students. A mutual chemistry and understanding. Which isn't the same as agreeing about everything."

IMITATION AND FREEDOM

> Read Lu Chi and make a poem.
>
> He doesn't say how it should be.
>
> Many had painted an oak before;
>
> Munch still painted an oak.

> Olav H. Hauge

2000 | I'm a student of music at Voss's upper school and am on a bus from Voss to Granvin to have a session with Knut. In our previous session I was taught "Bygdatråen," an unusual and wistful tune notably played by Nils Mørkve, who came from Voss. I was utterly spellbound by this fiddle tune when I first heard it, and have lived and breathed in time with its dark-green notes for a week now. I cannot wait to play it for Knut. As we sit there in one of Granvin's preschool classrooms, I tune my fiddle as precisely as I can manage. After all, nothing less will do for the strange fiddle tuning used for "Bygdatråen." Knut finds tuning boring, and asks me instead:

"So, have you read any nice poems recently?"

"No, not really."

"I recommend you take a look at Olav Hauge's 'Lu Chi' poem. Maybe you could think a little about why Edvard Munch still painted his oak, despite all the oak paintings that came before him. Then we could talk about it next week."

I nod and start to play. All of a sudden in the middle of the piece, Knut grabs my bowing hand and cuts me off, making me jump. Then he says:

"That was such a beautiful ending to that section of the tune. Could you teach it to me?"

"What do you mean? Wasn't I playing it just how you taught me?"

"No, not quite, but that doesn't matter. I think it was a fine variation. I'd like to learn it. That is, if you don't mind?"

"Erm, well...sure!"

"But remember to give your bowing room to breathe and expand. Just like Edvard Munch's pencil strokes. Yes, that's it! Picture Munch's *Madonna* in your head, then play through 'Bygdetråen' one more time."

"But I can't remember what was different about my playing."

"That's great. Then come up with something else."

"To give your sheep or cow a large, spacious meadow is the way to control him."

Shunryū Suzuki

As a teacher, Knut is rarely categorical, and revels in giving multiple answers to one and the same question. It would never occur to him to declare the "correct" way of playing a fiddle tune. He gives high praise when something is played well, even if played differently to how he would have done it. Good music is good music. As Knut would say, taste is uninteresting. If he ever noticed someone needing help with self-expression, then he would step in, but carefully, by discussing it together with them. When it comes to teaching the craft itself, Knut is firmer and more concrete.

"Before I started teaching I decided that if I ever had a student, I would never try to steer their own artistic development. I would only ever *see* the student in a most attentive way, no matter what they were playing. I also thought it was important to rid myself of any thoughts about my duty to pass down a musical heritage. I wanted my students to feel free, and didn't want to weigh them down with all the responsibility I had experienced when I was growing up. But the way I give such diverse answers has also given rise to heated discussions. Some students think it has done them a lot of good, while others are less fond of it. Perhaps it depends on what stage of life a student is in. When you are young, you are usually obsessed with the idea that everything your master says is gospel. But I am after the opposite."

What about those students who blindly follow their master's advice?

"In those cases the only thing that will grow is the master's ego. If this is happening, then it is the master's responsibility to break it off with the student. Even I have worried about living vicariously through my students. That's why all the advice I give is mostly relevant only to the individual. I welcome innovative thinking and playing with open arms, and many of my students know what they want for themselves."

What if your students deliberately just want to play like you? As long as it's their own choice, is that okay?

"Whether they want to play like me for a bit or for their entire lives, I have no problem with it as long as I'm not the one pressuring them to do so."

I have sometimes felt that you aren't willing to admit just how much of an influence you actually have on your students.

"I must confess that's true, of course. But sometimes I notice my students becoming wary of my influence. Especially if they have been compared to me too many times. That's why I have occasionally found myself toning down myself as a teacher in front of certain students, encouraging them instead to seek other master fiddlers. It's sad when this happens. But these days, there is a strong demand and urge to free oneself from one's master, and the 'Folk Music Police' are watching over you. They mean well, but they aren't always wise.

"You also have to ask yourself: What are you actually freeing yourself from? Are you trying to free yourself from your history? From your heritage? Or are you simply trying to free yourself as a way of shirking your responsibilities? It might be just as liberating to copy your master, playing exactly like him and being guided by nothing but his influence. On the other hand, it wouldn't be that nice if all of my students were copycats. Someone once pointed out somewhat derisively that they had noticed a tendency in Hardanger, and most of Western Norway, of fiddlers playing like me. Even if this was true, it wasn't a good thing for me to hear. Personally, I think that the students I have influenced the most have been truly diverse. This has become more and more apparent to me as the years go on. Many flowers have blossomed into many colors. It makes me really happy that they have turned out this way."

I think this is also based in the fact that it takes a long time to move on from your master. It's been like that for me, anyway. Becoming daring enough to trust my own artistic choices as good decisions, regardless of whether you, as my teacher, agree with them or not. Maybe some people are destined to be copycats, while others will always rebel against you. In any case, I think there is no escaping the fact you have given the world something of tremendous artistic value, and so it is no wonder people have the urge to play music like yours. Don't we always strive to create something that resembles what we personally deem to be beautiful?

"This is due to a combination of time, how long you have been playing, and how well-known you become. Can we ever become our idols? Or is there a communal value, some kind of common structure of expression that bridges our individual differences? A mutuality we no longer think is there?

"I have often thought that people like us are so fortunate. We get to work with our unique, local folk music, cultivating something from the place we come from. I am often baffled that so many in Norway seek out an art form that is so far from home. Is their local culture less important to them? Perhaps they don't identify with it? Is it something to do with us being such a young nation? Why have Norwegians placed so much more focus on America than Europe? All of this comes and goes in waves anyway, just like everything else. First you cultivate it, then you distance yourself from your own culture, only to go back again to cultivate it."

In which case, perhaps it isn't so much of an issue that a generation of Western Norwegians are playing similarly to you.

"No, I suppose that is the answer."

PERSPECTIVES AND PSYCHOLOGY

"This task will last your entire life." That was what Anders Kjerland said to Knut when he started teaching, which Knut took to mean that he didn't have to hurry with his students. He was pleased to hear this, since Knut is a strong believer in letting things come naturally. He believes that a master needs to keep an open mind and let the students guide their own teaching. They have their own tempo without being aware of it, and their teacher should adjust themselves accordingly.

"I could never bring myself to bully my students into developing a 'correct' fiddle technique. Force isn't a good motivator when you want to bring out the spiritual side in your students, but it doesn't necessarily suppress it, either."

So, then a master needs to have a good idea and intuition of when to give someone a push or not?

"In order to be a good teacher, you need to be psychologically aware of how your students' minds work, and it takes a long period of time to develop that knowledge. If you push a talented student too soon, then too much stress, high expectations, and nerves could bring their development to a screeching halt. I've learned that the hard way."

But what can you do when a talented student doesn't realize their own talent? When they struggle to see the point of nurturing an innate gift that they don't even believe in?

"Anytime I notice this happening, I feel a strong urge to step in. But even though it might take many, many years, a student will eventually figure it out for themselves. A student's self-development will take as long as it has to. Only they can lead the way. As their teacher, you have to help guide them, but you must never try to change people."

Then what yields the best results in teaching?

"Going slowly. And being almost invisible to my students."

Knut believes that, given time and luck, master-student relationships can often go beyond standard teaching relationships, and you can become dependent on them. That regardless of the student's age or artistic capacity, you will establish a bond with them. But Knut warns that the hardest challenge in these kinds of mentorships is keeping your feelings in check. Things become difficult when students begin asking themselves: "Does my master like me? Am I good enough for my master? Or are his other students better than me?" The opposite can also happen, when the master becomes hurt and angry because his student wants to study under someone else. Or when the master sees it as a personal attack if his student wants to play differently from him.

"Even though it might occasionally feel wonderful, I don't always think it's wise to mix work and friendship. A master has to learn to hold back. Although each master-student relationship might vary in how successful or unsuccessful they are, this is just something a teacher has to live with. When human beings are involved, there will always be challenges. In some cases, for example, students of mine have unexpectedly cut ties with me as their teacher and authority. Students occasionally turn their back on their masters in search of artistic independence. I did the same to Anders Kjerland. But after a while they tend to return, which is when a master *must* make sure to welcome them back with open arms. I set personal restrictions when it comes to making friendships with my students, but never when it comes to sharing music. A master has to bear in mind that they are in service *to* the student, not the other way around."

Has a student ever become jealous of you?

"No, never of me. More of their peers. Many of them would like to have the limelight to themselves. But it all boils down to generosity. It has to be completely present. Many forces nowadays will tempt us away from this, which is why it takes so much time to learn to become truly generous."

Knut believes you need to be ready to learn from your student when they are doing something better than you. In fact, his students have taught him more about teaching than anyone else. While this is true of his more mature students, it is especially true of his youngest ones, as they have no inhibitions. He believes that because children have such an unfettered freedom, they can come out with wonderful truths. Being "wrong" doesn't matter to them.

"They don't have a sense of property when it comes to art, either. Many people are close-minded about children, and end up cutting them off from a vast amount of resources. It is easy to underestimate children, too, because they don't have much life experience. You need to get to know children over a long period of time to truly understand their qualities. But this goes against today's target-oriented, result-driven philosophy."

I've often heard you say you prefer teaching girls to boys. Why is that?

"The emotional sensitivity I aim to build on in this art I find in greater percentages in girls than boys—at least within the age group I work with at the culture school. Girls are often less set in their ways and more emotionally mature. They are often wiser and have a greater sense of empathy. When I hear boys—and men—mocking girls for being 'goody two-shoes,' I often wonder if it stems from their own feelings of jealousy and regret. But the good (and rather ironic) thing about boys is that because they're not always as sensitive as girls, they have a different way of doing things. Boys put themselves out there and are strangely much more willing to take chances."

"Nowadays, a female quality has entered our tradition, as so many more women are playing the Hardanger fiddle over the last thirty years. Around the country there are probably more girls than boys playing today. For me personally, the feminine harmonizes better with music than the masculine. If a balance can still be found between girls and boys, I think that would be best."

CHANGE AND A NEW GENERATION

After teaching for such a long time, Knut has discovered that there are many different ways to learn the Hardanger fiddle. And despite students setting out from wildly different levels and backgrounds, their end results are just as good. Knut used to insist on bringing students along to *kappleikar*, but now he only does so if they ask for it. Over the years, Knut has slowly realized how important it is to preserve a child's innocence for as long as possible, before responsibility and critical thinking intrude and begin to control a student's mindset.

"In today's society and culture, everything is strongly oriented toward achievement. Great value is placed on having a career, and people feel pressured to rid themselves of anything that might obstruct their career path. I don't agree with that at all. On the contrary, these ideas can seriously restrict an artist's spiritual development. These days I take much more time to

talk to my students about being present in music. By that, I
don't mean being on a stage, when you feel present and absent
simultaneously. In a learning environment, in order to 'get there'
(in the words of Bjarne Herrefoss), you have to exist in the here
and now and feel at peace with that."

Over the years, Knut has noticed a change among his younger
students, for whom it has become much more challenging to
maintain concentration. It is also a struggle to find enough
time to practice. Knut believes that these days young people are
reluctant to set aside time and make their own decisions. For
this reason, he finds it helpful to encourage them to think about
what they want to do. Do they want to *really* master something?
To learn everything about a discipline? He also discusses with
them the difference between short-term and long-term goals.
Finally, he plays for them as well as he possibly can, to help
them preserve love for this music.

"I wouldn't ever go so far as talking about 'the golden days,'
but I do think things used to be a lot simpler. Generally, there
were fewer issues to worry about. Although nothing about our
true selves has changed in the slightest, the surface aspects
have. And now it is much more difficult to actually choose
something. Your soul just can't take it. If you want to learn to
play the Hardanger fiddle, you have to accept that it will take
a long time before you can hear any results. You have to be
ready to forget about other things for a long time, or else you
will never spend enough time with the instruments. The fiddles
expect nothing less, and they will make some nasty noises to
prove it!"

*A fellow musician once told me about a student he had, who was
wondering whether he could buy some drumsticks that could play
faster.*

"You can't help but crack a smile at stories like that. But it does say something sad about our society, about a tendency that goes far beyond a little boy wanting faster drumsticks. I have noticed that people feel like they are finished with education a lot sooner, and that they expect learning processes to take less time than they used to. But what are we doing to our young people if they never learn that it takes time to master an art and mature? I have also heard about students that stop visiting their master as soon as they are finished with their exams and formal education. How has this happened? I kept having lessons with all of my masters until their dying days, and they always had something more they could teach me."

Do you think there will still be room for this traditional master-student system in the years to come? By that I mean private initiative outside formal institutions.

"It will always exist. I am also convinced that, in the future, some people will be even more eager to dedicate themselves to a discipline like this one, precisely because the processes of today's society are so rushed."

Every year since becoming a teacher, Knut has always made sure to schedule his best students at the end of the day, so that afterward he is free to play with them as long as he wants. The culture school's head teacher and its students have no idea that he has been doing this for years, and that he does so free of charge. But Knut is convinced this is a necessary precaution if we want to expose the real gems of each generation. Knut has never stopped believing in the importance of culture schools, but thinks that they will soon have to change in order to survive.

"The institution has a beautiful philosophy behind it: that everyone deserves equal and affordable access to music, and that the teacher should always come to the student, not the other way around. But I believe that after a while, they should demand something from the students. They should be made to have a short exam or an audition after three years, for example. That would weed out any students who might only be going there for social reasons, out of habit, or because of parental pressure."

At certain points in his life, Knut has regretted not starting up a private school of his own when he was younger. This is because he has become increasingly convinced over the years that those who should have most say in issues over administration, curriculum, and best teaching practices *ought* to be the people with the most knowledge of the subject itself.

"That way, we could avoid all these conflicts between groups of people who come from different planets, who don't even speak the same language. Having said that, my many years of teaching have been tremendously rewarding, due to all the joy and maturity I see blossoming in my students. I am incredibly grateful."

And we are, too.

"Well, then. When both parties are grateful, it's definitely something worth saying thank you for."

TO BE NOTHING

1964 | The bus turns onto the narrow lane that connects Folkedal to Øvre Granvin. Only a few old wives and Knut ever drive this way on Sunday mornings. The white wooden church beams out across the verdigris landscape. The pealing of church bells rings out stronger and stronger as the bus approaches, and Granvin's lake softly mirrors the green and white shadows of its surroundings. Knut has heard so many stories about Jesus, about how kind he was to everyone he met. But Knut doesn't think too much about such things, and this isn't really the reason he comes out here every Sunday. He just wants to sit in this beautiful space and sing hymns together with all the other villagers who like being in the church. He loves listening to the organ, too. For a long time. It feels so good to be here in God's house by the lake. Here Knut feels safe. In church and together with his fiddle.

who is writing, is it me

or is it something that writes in me and

writes my writings

through me, perhaps it is I who write

if it is I who write

then there is an I who, each single time, is different, because

in the motion of the writing there is always

an I who writes and this I is not me

or perhaps it is me

but this I is so different each time

that it cannot be me

if it is I who write

then I am all these very different I

who still, in each writing is a distinct I, because

this is how it is: if I shall write

and be close to what is not

an I must be distinct

or noticeable in all its indistinctness

and this I is only present

in exactly what is or has been written and then it is gone

each writing has its own I

and without this I the writing loses its motion

and direction

this so different I, which is still so noticeable

this different I, which the writings create, and

which creates writing and

is a something and maybe it is this something the writing is
all about

Jon Fosse

(Translated by May-Brit Akerholm)

1999 | Khirbet Qumran is a ruined settlement northwest of the Dead Sea. Small oases of green palm trees soften the otherwise dry and barren wasteland, covered in ochre sand and stone. It is scorching hot. Knut plays a concert in Jerusalem and the day after gets the chance to drive out and see these desert ruins. Here is where at first a little shepherd boy and later a group of Bedouin shepherds in 1947 found the legendary Dead Sea Scrolls, hidden inside jars in the mountain caves. Altogether, nine hundred different religious texts regarding Jewish beliefs and culture were found, written back when the local *yachad* (Hebrew for "community") still existed. This civilization existed between 150 BC until the Romans came and destroyed it circa 70 AD. Debates about the nature of this ruined city bounce endlessly back and forth. The community was probably a seat of power of the Essenes, a pious religious sect that believed in ritual purification and communal property. Some people have postulated that the site may have been a monasterial community where people could devote themselves to spiritual learning. Others believe it may have been a kind of sanctuary for travelers, and that even Jesus and John the Baptist might have belonged to this Essenian community. But what the findings doubtless indicate is that Qumran was an important location for the collection, preservation, and production of sacred religious texts.

"The sight of Qumran's forts and ruins made an unforgettable impression on me. Standing there, surrounded by the cradle of civilization, a meeting point where all three of the world's largest religions have been worshipped by so many people for thousands of years, I felt strongly the interconnectedness of all humanity. It had never been clearer to me. This encounter with Qumran became an important turning point in my life, and afterward my self-image of being simply a medium for music became even stronger."

The hidden gospels of Qumran weren't adopted by the time the Bible took its final, more recognizable form. But reading through them, Knut discovered a religious message which resonated with the image he had had of Jesus since he was little—someone who was true and good, and free from prejudice. He also learned about the secretive Essenes, a sect of highly cultivated, elite masters of their discipline who handed down knowledge to their students in a kind of educational institution or guild.

Deep down, something in Knut has always resonated with religious thinking, but he no longer gets the same feeling from the church he once did as a boy, since a lot of the church's history no longer agrees with him. Yet his belief in spiritual power is as strong as ever.

"These days I feel more of a draw toward the beliefs of the Quakers: There is a light in all of us, and little pieces of God are in and around everyone. I also appreciate the fact they don't believe in preaching."

I have often heard you say that you are "a nothing." What do you mean by that?

"What I mean is that it isn't me playing, even though I'm the one physically making music. Something else is playing through me. The actual individual, in this case the *person* Knut Hamre, is unimportant. It is never about me, but an art that is much greater than myself. This is why I am a nothing."

So is it like being a medium?

"Sadly, the word 'medium' has a lot of different connotations and carries with it a certain prejudice. That's why I use it as little as possible, and replace it with the term 'a nothing.' My theory of an artist being a medium for something other than himself or herself can be difficult to comprehend if you only believe in individualism. But if you imagine yourself being part of a greater web, then it can provide you with a lot of meaning and comfort to think this way."

When Knut was younger, he read about the Norwegian guild system in the 1600s. According to his understanding, these guilds were fellowships of people working toward a common goal. Knut looked at Hardanger, especially Granvin, in the same way. All the fiddle players in his village and throughout the region belonged in a way, as they still do, to their own guild, which had dedicated centuries to the Hardanger fiddle: playing it, poeticizing it, then passing it on to the next generation. These fiddle pieces are common property, and each fiddle player's goal is to keep them rich and alive.

"If you think about everyone playing the fiddle as being a part of a larger community, then the need to compete with one another and shine alone will gradually fade away. It makes it easier to be generous."

I would hazard a guess that this would seem like a foreign concept to our corner of the world today, where individualistic materialism and the Me Generation run rampant.

"People feel a strong urge to preserve their personal freedom, and many are scared of acknowledging their origins. They would much rather be their own source of originality. This mindset frightens me. After all, I don't think I will ever be good enough to be my own source of music. That's why it is better to harvest ideas from other people, to use them, then pass them on. I remember one time Bjarne Herrefoss was playing at a *kappleik*. After the competition was over, someone told him: 'Your playing sounded just like Gjermund Haugen.' Bjarne replied, 'Thank you very much, that makes me happy to know.' If you share responsibility, then you share the applause. But many people forget to share the flowers when their ego and their need for personal glory take over."

Knut is a passionate follower of this doctrine, as was the Italian violin maker Giuseppe Guarneri (1698-1744), who used to sign his instruments with the initials *IHS* (In Hoc Signo), which roughly translates to "In His Honor."

"It is almost certain that Guarneri was dedicating his violins to the glory of God, and not to himself. Think about all the people who built churches in the Middle Ages. They might devote their entire lives to the project, and eventually die without ever seeing the finished construction. Yet they continued the work. This is how it is for the Hardanger fiddlers, too. A long, long line of fiddle players has already come and gone, but there are new ones who will go on playing even after I and every other currently living fiddler is dead."

Although you are interested in guilds, I know you aren't fond of hierarchies in any form. Traditionally, each guild would have a master craftsman who would sign his name on the works of all other guild members. Aren't you contradicting yourself?

"The idea of a guild is no worse than the madness of those who want their names on posters to appear in much bigger letters than the names of their fellow musicians! I like it when people forget their individuality and devote themselves to a cause. That's my philosophy. But within each fellowship, there *must* be room for individual thought and interpretation. People will always have their own idea about how something ought to be played. Some people might think they are closer to the truth than others, but that is impossible, and not very interesting."

It sounds like it would be hard to strike a balance between placing us in a guild while at the same time making room for individual perspectives and opinions.

"It requires both a broad perspective and true generosity. I don't claim it to be an easy task, but I believe strongly in the merits of such a system, as long as you manage to find the right balance."

FINGERPRINTS
IN THE MUSIC

Knut is a fiddle poet, a man who plays with music, improvises with it, and turns it into poetry. He also enjoys having a certain amount of routine in his life when he is practicing and honing his craft, but never when he is performing music. Then he has to feel free, lest his love and joy for playing get ruined in the long run. Many fiddle aficionados consider Knut to be a trailblazer in Hardanger, invoking both their admiration and frustration. Yet Knut has never aimed to provoke the establishment for the mere sake of it. He just plays his fiddle, as he always has and always will, with a flowing rhythm and intricate ornamentation wherever he can fit it in. It is always easier to talk about other people's musical style than your own. If you ever ask Knut why he plays the way he does, he always gives the same answer: "It just turns out that way." Knut's playing is not governed by rules and systems. Neither does he believe that traditional Hardanger fiddle music is solely for dancing. When he was younger, he would play for dances at countless parties and weddings, both alone and together with other fiddlers, for hours and hours, if not the whole night through. Yet playing at dances still feels like being in a straitjacket. He does his job, and does it well. But Knut much prefers to be emphasizing the alternative dimensions of a rhythm rather than just keeping time in a dance.

"My heart is not a metronome. It doesn't always have a steady beat, so I don't see why I should play like that all the time, either."

Knut is always searching for a style of expression that speaks right to the heart and transcends the rational and the intellectual. Above all he strives to play with a warm tone. A tone in which people can recognize themselves. It should have a storyteller aspect, too. Just like an actor tells a story inspired by a script, Knut tells a story with each tune he plays.

"My bow is my voice, as well as the voice of every player using bows, and this voice is a mouthpiece for personal dynamics and self-expression."

How do you go about telling a story through a fiddle tune?

"I start with the unique qualities of the music that are already there. I listen to a tune and use everything inside to draw people in and paint the most intricate picture of its mood possible. Because fiddle tunes are more abstract than a piece of text, they provide both listeners and players a greater freedom of interpretation."

Literature, especially poetry, has had a huge effect on Knut throughout his life. His passion for telling stories with his fiddle has led to him learning a great deal from spending time with authors and actors. Knut has taken inspiration from many different poems and pictures for his own art, particularly Chinese and Japanese poetry.

"There is something about these compact little haiku poems, the way they capture both the big and the small, the way the universal and the local are united as one."

Several times I have heard you say the word "inspiration" is not important for you. But isn't it important to be inspired when you want to create something, like a new fiddle piece? Or a new improvisation?

"Ah, but what is inspiration, exactly? Is it something that comes to us spontaneously? Or is inspiration something that helps the flow of spontaneity? Or perhaps the only way of creating something spontaneous is by using the knowledge we gain from hard, methodical work? I would lean toward the latter. I have never understood people who stand about waiting for inspiration to come to them."

So the way you play has changed over time?

"Absolutely. I believe many of my influences have come to me without me ever really thinking them through. Yet there are elements I have cultivated intentionally, such as melancholy. When I was in my twenties I was probably a little self-centered, and thought it was something that worked for everyone else, too. I think it was a sign of the times, especially in the 1970s. It was as if people thought they had to hit rock bottom before they could find something that was *real* enough, something sufficiently heartfelt and emotional. And what you feel stays with you, you cling on to it, as I did for a very long time. Nowadays I have stepped away from all that, and tried to become more interested in happiness again. Being happy isn't always a total waste of time, is it?"

How have you become more happy, then?

"Most of it came from trying out many different things over a long life. There isn't just one way of doing things."

What Knut calls the superficial qualities of music, like virtuosity and captivating technical skills, strike him as a display of dominance. He finds them to be entertaining for the eye, not the heart. What he likes best about music is its innate, soulful energy. Without it, the art form would be one-sided. He is convinced that anyone who wants to play a fiddle tune well must capture as many sides of life as possible: melancholy and laughter, sorrow and joy. He refuses to call a fiddle tune a masterpiece until it contains every one of these aspects, in addition to having a fully-realized form, a good and logical melody, an elegant structure, original variations, a burgeoning style of expression, and rhythmic ebbs and flows.

"Many tunes capture every one of these various layers of life, but one that I feel begin as a tiny newborn baby then develop into a fully grown adult, filled with wisdom, experience, and goodness is 'Vestlendingen' (The Westerner) by Halldor Meland. The opening theme is like a little lullaby and the end is in full bloom. I think this tune is worthy of the term 'masterpiece.'"

When he was between ten and fifteen, Knut was able to meet Halldor Meland several times together with the fiddlers Anders Kjerland and Håvard Kvandal. Halldor talked to Knut as though he were an adult man, and told him about the various concerns he had when he was playing, like making sure every aspect of life was in each tune. Knut would interrogate him about other fiddler players while they were together, and Halldor would respond with descriptions of fiddle players like: "Bah, he has no tone!" or "Oh, *he* has a tone!" It was clear that this was at the front of Halldor Meland's mind and therefore concerned him greatly.

Personally, I prefer the shorter fiddle tunes from Granvin. Mostly because many of them are played on more beautiful tunings in addition to the more common oppstilt bass *(tuned-up bass). But also because they suggest improvisations of a completely different order than* Vestlendingen. *The structures are more open, whereas* Vestlendingen *already contains so much.*

"'Vestlendingen' has such a strict form, it practically *craves* interpretation. But I also need those Granvin tunes, precisely because they are so near and open, making you feel like a child delighting in play itself."

Interpretation, as with a classical piece?

"Yes. Or with a text. You don't just go about rewriting Henrik Ibsen's *Ghosts*. Instead, you interpret it. And you definitely don't paint over Leonardo da Vinci's *Mona Lisa*, either. Do you see what I mean?"

Yes, I do. But many of Granvin's pieces contain only a handful of sections that repeat themselves over and over, with tiny variations. These might prevent the newborn baby you were talking about from ever blossoming. I don't think these tunes have enough in them. The story is too short, and might never become anything more than just baby's cry. Is this kind of music worth less in your eyes?

"Maybe some tunes are meant to stay childlike and simple? To me, these are just as essential. But like I said, I find a melody to be most complete when it has both of these elements."

Knut appreciates resistance in his music, and seeks it in everything he does. Music needs to have a message, one that grabs hold of you and doesn't let go. It can't be too comfortable. Otherwise, it becomes dull. In the 1990s, when Knut's musical life was in its most meditative period, he would seek out fiddle players he knew were the opposite of him, such as the Voss fiddlers Trygve Hæve and Torleiv Gjernes. These were sharp, rational, down-to-earth musicians who played the fiddle well and in a way that mirrored how they lived their lives. When Knut was together with them, he would play in the same way.

"That way I managed to get a little input from the more grounded side of fiddle music. At the same time, it helped me find out exactly what was and wasn't important to me when it came to my own art. I think such resistance is necessary when we practice this art of playing the Hardanger fiddle, especially when there is so much temptation to spend time with people who agree with us all the time, and who praise and appreciate us."

THE BOWING HAND

The fiddler's bowing hand is his pen and pencil. With it, he tells the story of each tune. This is why bowing technique and bows themselves are an endless subject of debate among fiddle players. Bows have changed gradually over the past three or four centuries—from the shorter, lighter convex-shaped bows of the Renaissance and the Baroque to what is now called the modern bow, which is much longer and heavier and has a concave stick. The latter bows are the standard in European classical music, slowly growing in popularity through the 1800s up to the present day. We can tell from photos that a change occurred among Norwegian traditional fiddle players toward the close of the 19th century. You would often see them carrying "modern" Hardanger fiddles of the 1800s in one hand and the longer, classical bows in the other. Meanwhile there were also fiddlers carrying 1700s Hardanger fiddles, probably made by the "Botnakarane,"[11] together with the *tunnebandbogar*—"barrel-hoop bows" or "round bows," as fiddlers once called them— which are closer in appearance to the Baroque bow. The type of fiddle, strings, and bows one chooses to play with affect the overall sound. This has given rise to endless debates. The Voss artist and fiddler Magnus Dagestad (1865-1957) had this to say in defense of the round bow: "It is the only correct choice for the Hardanger fiddle and for our music! That is well-known. To bow with the *flatfele* (violin) principle is the path of the wayward fiddler."[12]

By the *flatfele* principle, Magnus Dagestad was referring to a classical bowing technique that first arose in the Romantic era. The violinist Ole Bull is perhaps the one to blame (or thank) for this new bowing style, which became popular among many traditional fiddlers in the second half of the 1800s and is still prevalent today.

When Knut was establishing his own bowing style, the German school of violin playing, led by esteemed fiddler and violinist Sigbjørn Bernhoft Osa, ruled the roost among Norway's fiddlers. The style involved holding a long, modern violin bow at the very low end of the stick and mostly focusing on a slow, legato bowing. Sigbjørn was convinced that this was the correct method, and paced around the group rehearsals of different Folk Music Associations around the country to help correct the technique of other fiddlers.

"I even received letters and comments from him in the post, after he came across a picture of me in the papers holding my bow slightly askew. He had scribbled an arrow over the picture, along with the question: What kind of bowing hand is this? His theory was that the classical Romantic style was more important than anything else. But today, I think my bowing is more like Halldor Meland's."

Perhaps this new, Romantic style of bowing doesn't always listen to the wants of the fiddle tune itself, as you were talking about earlier. A lot of the music from Hardanger probably comes from a lot earlier than the 1850s, meaning the majority of it was composed with shorter bows in mind. Surely the type of bow people use could greatly change how a tune can be played?

"Both Ola Mosafinn and Olav Håstabø used short bows right up until the end of the 1800s, so the trend obviously lasted a long time. But the Romantic style of bowing became so popular and widespread during the 20th century that it probably led to a simplification of the rhythms in our traditional music. This new style was the complete opposite of the styles used by generations that preceded it, who held their light bows higher up the stick for example. This reduces weight in the hand, which helps accentuate the rhythm of the bow's strokes much more than what the legato strokes of the long, modern bow invite you to do."

Halldor Meland seemed like someone who was right in the middle of two bowing styles, and you can hear clear traits he inherited from his teacher, Ola Mosafinn. Particularly in his triplets.

"True, and if you inspected the bow he used, you would notice that the part of the wooden stick just above the pad was well worn. In other words, contrary to the technique I was taught by Osa, he held the stick higher up the bow, which changed the sound and rhythm. The same went for Torleiv Bjørgum from Setesdal, who was part of the generation after Meland, as well as Anders Kjerland."

What about you? I know you've used a few shorter Baroque bows in recent years, but it seems like you are still loyal to the modern bow.

"I am, but now I have completely stopped using heavy bows. Right now I have a lightweight German bow from the early 20th century. This type of bow has become such a part of me that I would lose aspects of my own playing style if I crossed over to the shorter, lighter Baroque bows. I wouldn't be able to create enough energy with them, or enough of a draw to call out the tone of the instrument and make it sing and come to life in my hands. It's just two different bowing ideals providing two distinct forms of self-expression. In addition, the type of bow you go for is determined by the fiddle you're using. Many Hardanger fiddle makers around the turn of the 19th century preferred the violin with its strong and powerful sound. The renowned Oslo-based fiddle maker of the period, Gunnar Røstad (1874-1947), made Hardanger fiddles in the manner of Guarneri. I play one of these Røstad fiddles, and it goes without saying that if you want to take full advantage of an instrument like this, you need a certain weight in your bow and bowing hand to make it really sing."

Naturally, you have listened to a lot of Romantic-era classical music ever since you were a child. Presumably this affected your playing?

"In all honesty, when I was a boy I listened to everything I could lay my hands on. But sure, most of all I liked the great violin soloists at the time, such as Jascha Heifetz, Yehudi Menuhin, and Isaac Stern. And what fascinated me was their flowing, legato bowing, conjuring up vast moods that merged the cries of a baby and the voice of an adult into a single expression. They could create a grand world with a single stroke."

A SOARING MUSIC

How do some fiddle players manage to make their playing soar? As Torgeir Augundsson ("Myllarguten") was said to do, or Bjarne Herrefoss in his best moments? What makes music go beyond impressing to *moving* its listeners? So much so that they want to cry out in sheer ecstasy for more when they realize that it's over, as tears pour down their cheeks? Why can only certain fiddlers achieve this, even when another fiddler, who plays to impress their audience, might have a much better grasp of technique? Such questions have always fascinated Knut. Jon Fosse has used the Hungarian expression "an angel who walks across the stage" to describe moments when the theater manages to capture that same soaring sensation.

As Olav H. Hauge once put it: "The craftsman can, but the artist must." Knut believes this statement contains an element of truth, in that the artist needs a certain unrest in order to create art. This unrest separates great art from mere craft. Yet a good craft is still of immense importance to Knut. It is something for which he harbors deep respect and admiration. This is why a good craftsman doesn't deserve any less respect in his eyes. Indeed, he has spent his entire life improving and maintaining his own craftsmanship in the hopes of creating something that soars.

In your opinion, what do you need to make good art?

"The very first step: your fingertips should know your craft. You need to develop an outstanding technique, have a wide and varied backlog of repertoire to make use of, as well as a broad historical awareness of different fiddle players, playing styles, and instruments. You obviously require good knowledge, solid and tangible, of the art form you are working with. Generally, as a string player, without a solid foundation in your craft, you can only ever dream of creating something that resembles art. In many ways, the person with better craftsmanship might be far more capable than the artist. Yet they will never produce art. This is something that drives many outstanding craftsmen completely up the wall! After all, you can never force out that *special something* from sheer hard work. This requires the opposite: to become a channel for art to travel through you."

And once you know your craft?

"Then you need to forget about being good at playing, which is a strong driving force for many people. That's just dreadfully boring. But the way I see it, when all is said and done, the main difference between an artist and a craftsman is that an artist has the gifts required to make his art soar."

And Asle takes a gulp of beer and gives the mug back to Pa Sigvald and then he sits down on the stool and he puts the fiddle in his lap and plucks the strings and tunes the fiddle and then he places the fiddle on his shoulder and he begins to play and it doesn't sound too bad and he keeps playing and people begin to dance and he keeps playing and pushes on, he doesn't want to give up he just wants to keep going, he wants to force out the pounding grief, he wants the grief to become light, to lighten and lift up, to take flight and flow upward without weight, he'll make that happen and he plays and plays and then he finds the place where the music lifts and then it soars yes, yes, yes it soars yes and then he doesn't have to keep playing, then the music is soaring above all by itself and it's playing its own world and everyone who can hear, they can hear it...

Jon Fosse, excerpt from *Wakefulness*

(Translated by May-Brit Akerholm)

"For me, soaring happens without any regard for time or place, when everything is just right. Despite having lived a long time, I can count on one hand the times when I've experienced real soaring onstage. It's exceptional, in other words. I'm not sure what this soaring even is, yet I always know it when I hear it. As something familiar and universal at the same time."

Personally, I feel like I have felt this ascent strongest when I am completely alone with my fiddle, especially after having played continuously for a number of hours. Perhaps you can call forth this soaring by entering into a kind of hypnotic state, or a kind of trance?

"Then you would have no preconceptions. I've experienced a great freedom during these solitary moments, too."

This soaring might only last for a brief musical moment, and then disappear.

"True, it is a state where everything is beautiful. And once you feel this soaring, the magic of art, then you will always want to return to it, again and again. It will become a state you strive toward, for better or worse."

For worse?

"Of course, if you purposefully aim to achieve the sublime, then you're bound to be disappointed. You need to be in a state of deep concentration to be able to free yourself from yourself. Only then can the soaring begin. I also feel that, in a concert setting, you need to really love your audience for it to happen. Onstage fears and worries about proving yourself never allow your music to soar."

But what about soaring in others? Have you ever experienced that?

"Of course, many times. In those moments, the soaring opens all my senses and everything becomes more intense—almost unbearably so. Tears pour out, and I might feel like I am no longer in complete control of myself."

I remember Jon Fosse once said that grief is a prerequisite for soaring. If art and life are to combine to form something light and soaring, then there must have been some contrast and conflict beforehand that sparked it. What's your opinion, Knut?

"Is grief more powerful than joy, then? That would soon lead to people thinking an artist needs 'a little pain' to produce something worth more. And that doesn't quite sit right, at least with me. As I see it, a prerequisite for soaring is your mind being both sensitive and receptive, and being able to feel the pain of living, both for yourself and others. It isn't necessary for the artist himself to be the personal victim of suffering all the time."

Can soaring last over extended periods? Sometimes people look back on artists' masterpieces and say such and such an artist was "at their peak" during a certain period in their life, giving their best concerts, making timeless recordings, and so forth.

"Maybe some people harbor this soaring inside of them for a long time, and others only for a moment? Or perhaps a momentary soaring can put in motion a long and productive working period?"

Knut believes that artists rarely think of what they create as being of use for anything. For the most part, art's only function is to be *released*. An artist captures the ethereal, the spontaneous, the things that speak directly to the heart. But even artists don't make art all the time. It happens once in a blue moon, perhaps only ever a single time in a single painting, and then every artwork before or since suddenly feels like nothing more than good craftmanship. Or maybe it only ever happens on one recording, and then ten years pass before you can come close to creating anything like it again.

"I have also heard various literary scholars claim that only three or four poems by Olav Nygard can be considered as finished, well-rounded art. The same goes for fiddler Eivind Mo. He achieved great, special things with his music when he was young, but then perhaps thirty, or even forty years passed before he was able to reach that point again."

ON DRIVE AND FLOW

"I should probably go up to my chair and wring myself out," the author Tarjei Vesaas said one morning, before starting out on a long period of writing. Knut says that some artists like to fuss over their creations for a long time, while others work quickly and spontaneously, and can tell right away whether their work is on the right track or not. An example of this would be Hardanger fiddle makers Håvard Kvandal and Anders Aasen (1909-1985). Both were masters of their craft, having produced some of the country's best Hardanger fiddles. But ever since Kvandal discovered a set of techniques that worked every time, his fiddle-making methods plateaued for the rest of his life. The fiddles produced by Anders Aasen, his fellow craftsman in Eidfjord, on the other hand, were fresh and different every time, even if his last fiddle may have been his best one yet, usable as a model for later productions. Kvandal had been happy to create the same work over and over. Something that would have been unthinkable for Aasen.

"And so we return to this essential restlessness in artists, something that Kvandal probably never realized Aasen had. The same restlessness Anders Kjerland never realized that both I and Halldor Meland had. If you don't have this driving force from the outset, one that compels you to keep going, then you are lacking a crucial force for creating good art. This restlessness will be reflected in your art and give it tension."

Knut believes that a strong drive may not always be good for your art. On the contrary, it can push you too far toward thinking about wanting to play so well, for this or that reason, to be a success. Or you might obsess over a certain person liking what you do. Someone might feel driven to be exciting, groundbreaking, and different. Yes, people have many drives. Others might want something on your behalf, and then you will get exactly the same results. In art you need to have a constant flow, without any of these limitations. Pablo Picasso once said: "I have nothing to paint, yet I paint still." Knut interprets this to mean that you just have to keep making art. Paint, play, and write until suddenly this *something* just happens.

"Drive is the opposite of flow. But a drive isn't always damaging, at least not at first. It only becomes detrimental when it's strong enough to restrict you."

Knut has his own drive to start new projects and get people involved in them. He doesn't sit around for a long time thinking them over, but likes to telephone people the moment he comes up with an idea. This isn't always just the people from his own immediate field; it might just as well be singers, fiddle makers, or others.

"This has been an indispensable source of creative energy for me. Once again, it touches on my thoughts about guilds: that we are all within one artistic fellowship, working our whole lives toward an optimal form of expression, only to pass it along to others. This makes it essential to get as many people involved as possible: writers, poets, composers, fiddle makers, painters, singers, and whoever else. Then our guild might truly blossom. In this case, the more driving forces the merrier."

After all, was there not a naturally driving force behind Tarjei Vesaas wanting to go and wring himself out on his chair?

"Of course. But to write such beautiful novels as *The Birds*, you need to be able to forget yourself, too."

Chagall: Death

Light candles and take from night

its sorrow, as the fiddler

takes music from God!

Gunvor Hofmo

In Ancient Greece, music was perceived as the highest of art forms because people believed that music could cure illnesses. It was a means of purifying and bettering ourselves as humans, thereby bringing all of society into harmony. Similar schools of thought are found in China, and in India people are still taught that sound *is* God. Through the hypnotic effects of their music, many fiddle players elevate themselves above and beyond the rational plane until they reach a mental state where it is said you must forcibly remove the instrument from a fiddler's hands to get them to stop playing. The Hardanger fiddle's *slåttemusikk* is typically associated with dances, but the instrument used to be played at ceremonies honoring important transitions in life, such as weddings or wakes. Throughout history, there have also been considerable changes in the objectives and applications of music. Yet music has always been used as a remedy for physical and psychological ailments.

2002 | It is late evening and Knut is alone in his sitting room, playing his fiddle. This is his favorite time to play: when everyone and everything is sound asleep. The sky is clear, the mountain is black, and the fjord is still with its quiet blue hum.

Knut is busy losing himself in a melody, when he is abruptly cut off by the ringing of the telephone in the hallway. Knut stops playing at once, worried that something must be wrong to warrant such a late call. He picks up the receiver.

"Hello?"

Silence on the other line.

"Hello? This is Knut. Is anyone there?"

After a long wait, he hears a voice: "I need to hear a tune. I feel under the weather. Could I trouble you to play something for me? Just a little, over the phone?"

Knut has no idea who is calling, but he walks out to the living room, fetches his fiddle, and returns to where the telephone sits waiting. He plays a few comforting melodies to soothe the caller. Once he has finished, Knut picks up the phone.

"Thank you so much," whispers the caller, then hangs up.

MUSIC BEYOND FUNCTION

Over the years, Knut has had many listeners of his music, both friends and strangers, approach him for help. Many of these listeners are battling mental illnesses and tell Knut how his playing calms them and brings them peace. Others have said that hearing him play helps them see things from a wider perspective. It enables them to open up difficult memories and emotions they have kept shut off for a long time. His listeners tend to approach him after a concert, but they also send letters and emails. A few have even called Knut personally to hear him play over the telephone, or simply have a conversation.

"Later, I realized that my solo album *Fargespel*, which I recorded in 1993, had helped people. But it is particularly at concerts, when our communication is most direct, that my music has most likely had the biggest influence."

I've heard several people talk about your CD Fargespel *for this very reason. For example, one of your other students, Lajla Renate Buer Storli, told me how her father, Harald Storli, used* Fargespel *as medication after suffering a stroke. Whenever times got tough, he would turn on your recording like clockwork. His daughter tells me that your music opens up his heart when he needs it most, so both sorrow and joy can emerge. Why do you think that's so?*

"Well, how do I put it into words? I can only say I am grateful for the music I impart to my listeners being able serve a higher purpose. In any case, it is a good sign of how music can move people beyond the realm of the rational and the functional."

It isn't just *Fargespel* that has helped Knut's listeners. The cassette he released in the mid-1980s, *Slik spelar Knut,* generated a similar response. Cellist Stig Valberg recalls his own experiences with the album:

I probably wasn't aware of this healing effect—at least not the first time I listened to the cassette Slik spelar Knut. *During a particularly difficult period in my life, when chaos and angst became more central, music, which had previously been my dearest possession, started being pushed aside. All my apathy and existential angst, whether I admitted it or not, allowed me next to no musical input. Yet during my worst emotional turbulence, there remained two musical beams of light to both "ground" me and provide me with something more—a spiritual connection to something beautiful, pure, and divine. I only brought two records into the mental ward. One of them was J. S. Bach's* Sonatas & Partitas for Solo Violin *with Sándor Végh and the other was* Slik spelar Knut *with Knut Hamre. I think both of them had a spiritual and physical energy, as well as a clear structure and rhythm that, in those days, I dearly*

A double wedding outside Granvin church in 1895.
The famous fiddler Olav Håstabø is also there, back row, third from the right.
This is the only photo we could find in which he appears.

needed to survive. I know this might sound a bit over the top, but looking back, I know it's the truth. I am grateful that art is so vibrant and can offer so much to people in need—Pablo Neruda once said something about "Art is there for those who need it." I am grateful that Knut's music accompanied me into and out of my darkest days. Thank you!

Stig Valberg

What do you think about these total strangers contacting you and offloading their personal problems?

"Once you've been playing the fiddle for a while, you slowly realize that when playing music, you are doing so for the benefit of others. You become a kind of musical therapist. But I am still very aware that I can't perform any other role than the one I have. I can't pretend to be a psychologist or some kind of spiritual advisor. I am only a fiddle player. Though I know well what the power of music can do to people. But it's also important to me that playing the fiddle is something normal and mundane."

Olav Håstabø, a fiddler from Granvin, has also experienced his music being used to alleviate grief and rage. Once, at a wedding, the guests' tension and alcohol intake escalated to such an extent that a fistfight broke out. The guests then called for Håstabø to start playing, and the fight dispersed. He had played away their aggression.

When Knut was in his early twenties and had started playing for crowds rather than just his own pleasure at home, he realized that his music could occasionally serve a similar purpose.

"It wasn't something that was talked about in everyday life, so I lacked knowledge in the subject. Yet little by little, I realized that my music was performing a function that went beyond my own pleasure. It didn't change the way I played, but maybe my charisma changed, precisely because of this newfound awareness."

Nils Sletta, an actor and fiddle player, told Knut an anecdote about his mentor, Ola Løndal, with whom he had teamed for a folk music competition (*kappleik*). After finishing his tunes for the judges and audience, Ola strode out into the farmyard outside and sat down on a tree stump, as if in a trance, ready to carry on playing. Another fiddler, Jørgen Tjønnstaul, followed close behind. Tjønnstaul then fell to his knees in front of Ola, almost paralyzed, thrust his fingers into the dirt and smeared it over his face, while tears came streaming from his eyes. Ola didn't bat an eyelid. He just kept playing and playing, while Nils Sletta watched it all unfold from a distance.

"Every now and then, a kind of transformation can happen to a fiddle player, if they lose themselves in the soaring and become nothing. In these remarkable moments, a fiddler might oscillate so radically between the normal and the divine that eventually, even some shy weakling could walk out from backstage and immediately end up transforming something within himself and his audience."

During these moments, what kind of inner processes are taking place?

"You can't put them into words. They're abstract, but also close and familiar. If we could only see them, we would know that these experiences are completely normal parts of our daily lives. But these days, we have become so solely preoccupied with what is rational that only the things we can prove scientifically carry weight. That's why incidents such as the one with Ola Løndal in a trance and Jørgen Tjønnstaul on the ground in front of him seem strange and unbelievable to us now. But life can't always be explained. And when these experiences *do* occur, you have to respond to them with complete generosity and set yourself aside. You have to offer everything you have."

"We don't need to play loud. The world is loud enough."

Steve Tibbetts

1998 | Knut Hamre received an unexpected letter from jazz guitarist Steve Tibbetts. Steve had listened to Knut's album, *Fargespel*, back home in America and wanted nothing more than to take a trip to Hardanger, together with his longtime percussionist Marc Anderson, in order to make a recording with Knut. Not long after, Tibbetts and Anderson crossed the North Atlantic and made their way to the Hardangerfjord. The recording, which also features Knut's student Turid Spildo, was carried out over a two-week period at Utne Parish Church. During this time they took the daily ferry over the fjord from Kvanndal, going into each recording session without agreeing on or rehearsing anything beforehand, instead allowing their instincts to guide them. This recording would go on to become the album *Å*. The renowned music magazine *Billboard* was among the many publications to award this record a glowing review. In Norway, however, no one would distribute it or host concerts with the group. The record was regarded as unconventional. But it had to be that way.

"The only thing we had in mind was that the music could be a means of psychological and spiritual healing. Through music, one could strike back against aggression and conflict, and the warmth of the music might heal you."

Steve Tibbetts and Marc Anderson were, and still are, practicing Buddhists, and they associated their musical expression with their belief and its principles of anti-materialism. This had a natural influence on the way they chose pieces for the recording. When they couldn't find what they were looking for in the *springar* tunes, they turned to *rull, lydarlåttar,* and *bruresláttar* instead.

"The way they thought about music was new to me. It was an eye-opening revelation. Recording music like that really made sense. It wasn't about pleasing anyone or seeking success and approval."

Weren't you already thinking along those lines when you recorded Fargespel?

"Å fortified an idea that had already been sown during my days recording *Fargespel*. My visit to the caves of Qumran the following year would cultivate this idea in a similar way. I had also become increasingly fascinated by Audun Myskja, a healer and specialist in family medicine. Not least because he has written about music's historical usage as a partial substitute for medicine, having carried out research within that very field. Thanks to Å, Qumran, and Audun Myskja, I have adopted these philosophical concepts as the foundation of my musical style. I continue to seek out melodies that lack aggression and tunes with a great deal of rhythmic freedom, so they can be freely repeated and altered. But all of this has been a natural, unplanned inner process."

It took me a long time to appreciate the culture that exists around the Hardanger fiddle and Knut's music. Several years after the release of the album we recorded together, I began to think that the Hardanger fiddle is best played as a solo instrument. There's a certain power the instrument has when it is played by a master, unaccompanied.

Before I came to Norway to record with Knut, I studied what I could about the Hardanger fiddle and its place in the folk mythology of Norway. There were stories of huldra, fossegrimen, and waterfalls. There were stories of fiddlers who made deals with spirits similar to the legendary pact Robert Johnson made with the devil at the crossroads in Clarksdale, Mississippi. Now, years later, it seems to me that a lot of this superficial, popular mythology obscures a deeper level of the music that is only revealed over time.

There are deep levels to Knut as well, levels that become evident after you've known him for a while. He's always been old, he's always been young. There is a kind of equanimity in him; a rooted feeling. What you see is what there is, but at the same time there are layers behind layers. When he laughs, he means it.

When he came to stay at my house many years ago my triplets were three years old and afraid of strangers. When Knut walked up the stairs in my house and came into the living room they were standing there, waiting for him. I said, "This is Knut." They all stared at him, unsure. Knut took off his jacket, put down his fiddle, and squatted down to greet them, right at their level. He paused and winked. It was like a tree bending over to meet them. They walked right over, and put their hands on him, smiling. I'd never seen that before.

The unity of Knut, his fiddle, and his music is something I haven't seen often in musicians. I don't know if music is medicine, or if it has healing power, but I know I have felt myself relax and healed in a fundamental way while walking in forests and climbing mountains.

Knut himself has picked up some kind of power from the land. He embodies the subtle, pervasive energy of nature in his music and his being. It is like hearing a tree sing.

Steve Tibbetts

Perhaps Steve Tibbetts is onto something when he writes that the Hardanger fiddle has a certain power when it is played solo. This way its core isn't covered up, it is laid bare, making it easier to carry out the healing functions of music.

"If there are a lot of visuals happening all at once on the stage, whether they be costumes, choreography, lighting, or special effects, then I suppose that, yes, it might move the focus away from healing, and toward other inner processes with their own benefits."

To Knut, it is the music's ability to heal that matters most, so his greatest desire is that his music will achieve it. Yet he believes it is pointless to value some genres of music less than others, just because they might not be as therapeutic. Knut believes that we all possess these healing powers, but perhaps not everyone finds it natural to channel them outward.

"There aren't any rules about which kinds of music can heal and which can't. It doesn't matter whether it is funny or sad, everything has equal worth and can have healing powers, as long as it's performed purely and from the heart."

But what makes your audience members approach you after a concert?

"There's no real way of knowing. Occasionally musicians can summon forth some potent forces, especially through qualities in music that go beyond the concrete. I'm of the opinion that the task of an artist is to share something that doesn't just speak to our rational self. And I hope deep down that music will soon reclaim the space it truly deserves. It can't just hum along in the background all the time. I don't think the permanent availability of today's music contributes to the art form. There's no hard work involved in accessing music anymore, and this affects its status, as well as the people who produce it. We are fighting now more than ever to free ourselves from music."

Turid Spildo, Knut Hamre, Steve Tibbetts, Marc Anderson.

ON STAYING TRUE
TO YOUR ART

"This fiddler (Per Bulko) played a lot better than me. But unlike me, he didn't get famous. It doesn't matter how good you are if nobody knows you."[13]

Torgeir Augundsson
("Myllarguten")

Many artists find it so tough to make ends meet while earning enough respect and acclaim that they wind up being forgotten. Pure artistry doesn't necessarily ensure that an artist will have a big enough audience to live off their creations alone. History has countless examples of this. Vincent van Gogh sold only one painting in his lifetime to an art dealer who happened to be his brother. Few understood or appreciated his broad brushstrokes of golden fields and sunflowers. Yet van Gogh still painted sunflowers.

The years between 1850 and 1920 were the golden age for Hardanger fiddle soloists. Torgeir Augundsson, also known as "Myllarguten," was one of the first to perform a typical concert with the Hardanger fiddle, together with master violinist Ole Bull. In his most active periods, he was able to earn a lot of money doing so. Many other fiddlers wanted to achieve the same thing, and one after another tried their hand: Lars Fykerud, Sjur Helgeland, Ola Mosafinn, Torkjell Haugerud, Halldor Meland, Ola Mo, Sigbjørn Bernhoft Osa, and more. For many of them, it worked out well. But the Hardanger fiddle has always lived in the shadow of the violin, and many fiddlers started adjusting their playing to sound like one. Looking at old concert programs, it seems that fiddlers in this period all shared much of the same concert repertoires, and they did a lot to appeal to the market of the time by sprinkling their concerts with short circus acts, for example, or using their fiddle to mimic cows, birds, and other sounds of the "simple shepherd's life."

Halldor Meland was against all such marketing ploys. He was a far-left radical, and would often say things like: "The birds sing better than I imitate them on my fiddle!" Knut believes there were many splendid painters during the late 19th century in Norway who sold out on their art by adapting it too much to suit the market. He tells the story of Nils Bergslien (1853-1928) of Voss as proof.

"He started painting fat, drunk monks and small elves of Norwegian folklore because his audience thought it was funny, yet I can't imagine it was what he really wanted to paint, deep down. It is essential we remember that it is not the mob who shall dictate to an artist what to make."

But is the artist ever truly free from the opinions of the mob?

"Perhaps not. Most who choose to live off nothing but their art, full-time, probably need to have a certain audience in mind, whether they are willing to admit it or not. Art used to be controlled by its patrons and by the church, but now it is dominated by the state and event organizers. Of course, this is all a different kettle of fish for artists who are financially independent."

Yes, and for those lucky enough get to work with a genre they love, that in addition comes with a large and loyal following audience who welcomes them with open arms. It is probably a lot harder to find this perfect balance if you work with what some people call the "narrower arts."

"The only advice I can give is that you need to make sure you remain as uncompromisingly true to yourself as possible, as to your art. We need to keep reminding ourselves about this our entire lives, especially now that the free market is so dominant. Remember, truly timeless art does not need a place to fit into society. If your work is of high enough quality, it will one day be discovered. You have to trust in it. Unfortunately, as in the case of van Gogh, you might have to risk dying before that happens."

I have noticed that quick results born of easy solutions soon develop into a dirty habit among many musicians. Some might start working on a project simply to maintain their current success, instead of it being what they truly want to do.

"In that case, I think this shows a lack of foresight. We can't always assume that if the audience claps, the artist has produced something of merit. If an artwork has achieved wide success, or if an artist appears often in the media, then most people will only clap because everyone else is clapping. Most of the audience will just follow the crowd, whether collectively slaughtering or honoring the artist. Only a slim minority actually enjoy feeling like outsiders. Thankfully, there are a few who dare to step out and say what they really mean. And if you ever venture to ask for the opinions of experts, then I am sure you will get a different response to politicians and the general market."

But isn't art supposed to be for everyone?

"In theory, it is for everyone, as long as they are willing to accept it. But if art is to survive, it needs to breathe freely. Art has to live with the people it *can* live with. I'll say it again, because it can't be said often enough: It is the artists themselves who must decide the nature of their art. Not their audience and not the organizers of an event."

But isn't it almost always the latter who decide?

"Yes, it happens over and over again."

So why don't we learn?

"Money and respect."

Should we be uncompromising or underfed?

"People have to decide for themselves what they want, and what feels necessary at different points in their lives. We need only remember not to just *stay there*. Art cannot blossom under any premises other than the ones artists put forward themselves. It cannot fall victim to public opinion, or it will just become another commodity to sell. Artists also need to be self-aware. What do you want? Where do you stand? You need to keep asking yourself these questions throughout your entire life."

But surely not everything that sells is bad?

"It's fine as long as the artwork is honest. You notice quickly whether something is true or pandering. Our own folk music is now beginning to teeter back and forth in this regard, and we need to keep an eye on ourselves. We have become greatly dependent on the voices within our own specialist environment and what messages they are sending to politicians and event organizers. Right now, it seems the goal is to appeal to as large an audience as possible, which can quickly cause us to lose what makes us unique."

STAGE FRIGHT
AND THE FEAR
OF FEAR ITSELF

Many musicians know this crippling anxiety about performing all too well, and it is rarely logical. You might be seized by anxiety seconds before you are due to play, or it might start around half a year beforehand. Certain people might seldom or even never be plagued by this problem, while others could be racked by stage fright for years. It might become so debilitating that it makes them turn away from art and pursue something else.

1985 | Knut's heart is pounding, hard. It feels like it is about to burst out of his chest, and his breathing doesn't quite seem to reach his lungs and stomach. He is waiting backstage at the Grieghallen concert hall in Bergen, a quivering hand clutching his fiddle and bow. Out in the auditorium, the crowd seems tense with expectation. Today, Knut is supposed to play a single fiddle tune as part of a larger event. Where he is waiting, many different fellow musicians rush in and out of their dressing rooms, warm up, stretch their arms, hum under their breath, and pace back and forth impatiently while they rehearse their lines, hastily and nervously. For months, not a day has passed without Knut going through this day in his mind, and he hasn't been able to sleep for the past couple of nights. But now the day has come, and he is sitting backstage, trying to breathe and not think, breathe and not think, breathe and not think, as his eyes dart nervously around the backstage area. He doesn't know where he is supposed to go. He doesn't want to be here, he doesn't want to play. He just wants to leave. Does he have to go out there, just to play this one little tune? No, he can't do it. Hell no! The other performers, who have just finished their acts, return with smiles of relief on their faces, whispering to Knut, "Break a leg!" A stage manager with a jabbering walkie-talkie on a loose cord around his neck comes over to him: "You're up."

Knut stands up automatically, trying to breathe and not think, and realizes that one of his feet has placed itself in front of the other. He takes sharp breaths and thinks, I can't do this, I don't want to do this, I'm not up to it, I won't get it right, my fiddle is out of tune, I'm going to fall to pieces, forget the piece, mess it up, play it badly, until suddenly he is standing in the middle of the stage under a solitary light.

Knut lifts up his fiddle and rests it against his neck, then takes out his bow. But neither the fiddle nor the bow feel like a fiddle and a bow anymore; they have turned into something else, something unrecognizable, and Knut can see his fingers moving and his arm bowing, trembling across the thin fiddle strings. He plays with his quivering bow until he reaches a point in the first section, when he freezes up and simply can't continue. His heart is pounding inside him. Knut plays it once more from the start, all the while dreading more and more reaching that same point, anxious that he might freeze up again.

Knut plays for the audience the first section of a tune he has played countless times since he was a boy. Then the moment he rounds off his final stroke, he rushes off the stage. His breathing is hurried, his body is shaking, and behind him Knut can hear the sound of applause slowly dying away.

PRESTIGE AND BEING NOTHING

This anxiety was both physically and mentally debilitating for Knut, and it made him feel like he was losing himself.

Today, Knut regards the entire 1990s as a period characterized by his struggles with anxiety. The absolute worst and most anxiety-filled years occurred between ages thirty-five and forty. It helped when his mind was stable, but when life got tough, he would start focusing on the negative things. And as this anxiousness burned away at Knut, he quickly developed a blinding fear of fear itself, which was an even worse condition. It was a madness.

"My fear of fear itself went so far beyond all common sense that I even started becoming nervous about playing at the old people's home in Granvin. Imagine that! Afraid of playing in front of all those senior citizens, sitting there listening with their hearing aids, some of whom were even half deaf! Everything you worry about going wrong will naturally go wrong if you start thinking like I was about standing on stage. It will eventually make you lose your appetite for playing music, which is a great grief."

On numerous occasions, Knut felt tempted to give everything up altogether. One day he drove down to the lumber mill in Granvin to ask whether they had any work going. He couldn't stand it any longer. There weren't any positions available. Somewhat ironically, Knut's anxiousness hit its peak when he was in his prime as a fiddler. He was receiving every kind of prize and commendation, winning *kappleikar*, holding lots of concerts, and had just been given a new position as County Musician (*Fylkesmusikar*) in Hordaland. Yet the more praise and glory he received, the smaller his self-worth became.

"I felt all these huge expectations upon me, which I knew I would never be able to fulfil. Yet I wanted so desperately to do so, to liberate myself from all of them."

In a way, it strikes me that you started experiencing this anxiety as late as in your mid-thirties. You were doing well as a fiddler long before that. How did you manage to hold it off at the beginning of your career, before you became so respected?

"Because I managed to remain naïve for so long. In my

twenties, music was still a sheer joy to me. Until I had this breakdown in my thirties, I never felt any kind of restrictions, guidelines, or needs compromising my music. As I said, this breakdown happened partly because I stopped being so innocent, but also because I had departed from music's original virtues, and had started to associate it with status, prestige, and personal glory. I also started being cast in roles I didn't feel at all comfortable with, which made me feel even worse."

It's interesting that so many people have described being soothed and calmed by listening to your solo CD, Fargespel, *given that it was recorded during the worst of your periods with anxiety.*

"When you are suffering from this anxiety, the energy you call forth during recordings and concerts like these can be immensely powerful. And the audience can probably sense that. In these moments, all sense of routine is swept away, and art made by routine has no place in the disciplines we're discussing. You need to do away with every disguise, and once you do, you dive right to the center. That way, I believe your music will still have a chance at healing people."

MENTAL CONTROL

Knut eventually realized that if he was going to keep playing the Hardanger fiddle for a living, he needed to do something about his anxiety. It couldn't go on this way, slowly but surely losing his appetite for fiddle playing—an activity that had provided him with an all-encompassing purpose ever since he was a little boy. So Knut had to find his way back to the original virtues of music: truth without compromise. He slaved away for several years, trying to turn his circular, negative trains of thought around. Yet the whole time, he had to remind himself about his true life philosophy: He serves the music, not the other way around.

"This was also the period when my 'to be nothing' philosophy started coming to the fore. It was unbearable to maintain a state of trying to be 'everything.' Therefore, it was much easier being 'nothing.' This philosophy saved me as a musician, and my life improved greatly because of it. Of course, it seems logical, really. If you are nothing, then you can't fail!"

In addition to these mental battles, Knut purposefully carried out other strategies to make things easier. At times he would only play tunes he knew were safe and easy, and that made him feel completely prepared to perform. When he was actually onstage, he might also focus on a single imaginary person in the audience to communicate with. He would imagine a person who was only there for Knut, and who loved and derived enjoyment from everything he did.

"This has worked particularly well because it enables me to direct all my energy to one specific person. The person I imagine tends to be a woman, since I feel that women are more selfless than men. It provides the energy I need to calm my stage fright and make good music."

To achieve this, Knut has to concentrate extremely hard and shake off any distractions about who is or isn't sitting in the audience, about whether he is sitting comfortably on the stool, whether there are any journalists or skeptical peers in the audience, whether his fiddle isn't set up right, whether he is going to hit a creative wall, or whether his anxiety will get to him. This is why Knut refuses to look at the audience while he is playing: so that he stays focused on the music alone. Knut also believes in the importance of making sure every practical aspect of an instrument is in order—from the strings to the tuning pegs—before coming onstage. Otherwise, this will take up all of your attention. There is always that old trick of arriving at the venue long beforehand, too. Checking out the stage and the sound of the concert hall, warming up, and picturing the concert in your head, so that nothing feels new when you're actually sitting there.

"When everything is in place, I turn myself into nothing, imagining all the energies outside of myself and all the people helping me, or that fictional, selfless person in the audience."

But what do you do if you don't believe there are any people helping you?

"Then you might have a problem, because that would mean that you believe you are the only person who can help you. In any case, you have to think about everything one step at a time. No matter what, you need to get rid of any thoughts about what happens once you've finished, about the critics, about whether people liked it or not, and so on. The moment I step onto that stage, that world no longer exists."

The few times I have truly played well on stage, I can scarcely remember even being there. There might be a few dim recollections of the beginning and end of a concert, but everything else is gone. Yet afterward, I still felt like something good happened.

"Yes! That is a truly pure, indescribable goodness! An emptiness, like you were deep in a great meditation. And I think once you've experienced something like that, then you have reached a state of being nothing. After all, if you manage to reach that point, then you must have been intending to disconnect yourself. This would push you into a kind of trance, and the key to getting there is having an unshakable concentration."

During these years, Knut also sought help and guidance from religion and his own theories about the Hardanger "fiddlers' guild." But the person who helped Knut the most of all was Olav H. Hauge.

"Olav did everything he could to soften his reputation as an individual. He was a great poet and philosopher, but he always told everyone he met that he was a gardener. I know he saw himself as a humble medium for his poetry."

To me, it almost sounds as though he clung to this gardener image because he was afraid of something, too?

"Olav was terrified that if the winds blew too much in his favor, then all his fine poetry would come to a halt. I remember that if he ever got a bad review, he would say it was really a good review because it would make him try all the harder. Hence why he cultivated his opposition, and wrote things like: 'praise is a poisoned chalice.'"

Do I sense a hint of self-flagellation in there somewhere?

"Oh, he definitely might have dabbled in that now and then; Olav was very strict with himself. But it is also true that we live in a nation where the infamous *Janteloven*,[14] a result of the competitiveness of society if you ask me, holds great sway over all of us. It probably affected Olav, too. But the main reason he thought this way was a growing fear that the weight of all his praise would soon grow too heavy and stem the flow of his writing. There can be no doubt that the main setback for artists is their ego."

Some people might feel aggravated by you saying this. After all, it's easy for you to say that you are nothing when you have been given every conceivable kind of affirmation to the contrary. It might be easier for you to think this way than for an unknown and unrecognized artist.

"I could see that. But didn't I already say how it made me feel when I started receiving all this acclaim for how good I was? My self-respect dropped even lower! Other people's praise does little to comfort our inner selves. It is just an illusion. If you get too enthralled by praise, then you soon become dependent on it."

This might be a naïve question, but don't we sometimes need praise, too?

"Of course, it can be positive to a certain extent, especially when you are young. It is all about balance. You need to live only for the mission, and preferably forget about the poet behind the work. Everything else is fleeting. When the poet is dead, the art will still remain. If it's good enough."

Might your 'to be nothing' philosophy also be seen as running from responsibility, and a form of escapism?

"I suppose, if you see yourself as being the center of things. It's just not for me, that line of thinking. Do you want to assume sole responsibility for everything you create? What about sharing your rewards and responsibilities with others? If you are trying to imagine yourself as nothing, then you need to realize that you depend on other people. There is nothing wrong with trying to soothe your own soul by creating good art, but you need to do it without any other objective in mind than making good art."

Do you think that you could personally improve?

"Of course, but I can't do it alone. I need help from the 'invisible hands,' as Jon Fosse phrases it in one of his poems, and that comes from faith, not hard evidence."

Faith in what? In God?

"Yes. Or at least a power greater than myself."

If you manage to lead your life according to these philosophies of being nothing and of being in service to music, then it must be an extremely liberating experience. You have encouraged me to do so for so many years, and I feel a great temptation and a will to try, but I think it is difficult to achieve in practice. At least all the time. I have thought that you ought to have some level of inner self-confidence, a kind of trust in the artist in you to start with, to help you think like that.

"No, feeling stable and self-confident to begin with won't make this 'nothingness' arrive any more naturally. You will only find peace by imagining yourself as nothing, thus encouraging you to peel away any dualistic notions about achieving something, pleasing everyone, and becoming better and better every time you perform. If you don't keep it in check, perfectionism can cut you off from what matters. The same goes for when people expect certain things from you, which makes you raise your own expectations of yourself. A perfectionist is never pleased, which is why we have to learn to love ourselves. Although this 'being nothing' is not a doctrine I encourage all of my students to follow, I do think it might work for you, in the long term. Perhaps an artist needs to go through certain milestones in life before they can realize this idea? Maturing as a human being takes time, and more time than we are willing to admit. But we need to allow ourselves and other people to give it time."

And yet all of us are socialized to think that we should accomplish things.

"That we are, but this socialization can also somewhat restrict an artist's freedom. They should instead teach people how to become human. After all, in our society we are not socialized by our philosophers, but by our politicians. The worth of human beings is measured in their achievements, and everything is dominated by individualism. Profits and rewards rule the day. It's no surprise that we break down. One thing I can be sure of is that, if I hadn't managed to turn around my way of thinking, I would have thrown in the towel as an artist. So really, I was rescued by learning to tone down my own individual worth and become nothing. It is only when you emerge and depart from yourself that poetry can appear. Goethe is supposed to have once said: 'Being yourself is so little.' You need to have a broad perspective, and for God's sake remember to laugh at your attempts. Self-irony can do a lot for untying mental knots. It's no good being self-righteous."

Many people turn to alcohol or medication to help cope with their anxieties.

"That is clearly a poor solution if you don't actually need medication. As I see it, the angst we are discussing here is caused by having a certain mindset. It is not the darkness we fear most, but the light. It is important that an artist thinks carefully over why they do what they do. Are you out for personal gain? Are you answering a call? Do you want to bring joy to others? To pass something on? Are you simply enjoying yourself? Or are you trying to please your event organizers, journalists, and peers? What do you want your music to mean to you and other people? What has your music meant for different people through time? I don't have the answers, but these are important questions."

What is music for you?

"A confirmation of everything that is beautiful. Music provides you with a clear sight, which opens up channels into yourself and intensifies the emotions that soothe you."

When the Shoe Fits

Ch'ui the draftsman
Could draw more perfect circles freehand
Than with a compass.

His fingers brought forth
Spontaneous forms from nowhere. His mind
Was meanwhile free and without concern
With what he was doing.

No application was needed
His mind was perfectly simple
And knew no obstacle.

So, when the shoe fits
The foot is forgotten,
When the belt fits
The belly is forgotten,
When the heart is right
"For" and "against" are forgotten.

No drives, no compulsions,

No needs, no attractions:

Then your affairs

Are under control.

You are a free man.

Easy is right. Begin right

And you are easy.

Continue easy and you are right.

The right way to go easy

Is to forget the right way

And forget that the going is easy.

Chuang Tzu

(Translated by Thomas Merton)

ANNLAUG BØRSHEIM

From Ulvik, born in 1982. Today, she works as a freelance musician, specializing in vocals, guitar, and Hardanger fiddle. She also occasionally works as a teacher of the Hardanger fiddle. Børsheim has two CD releases to her credit, and has mostly worked at the junction between folk music, pop music, and Norwegian folk songs. She has led a solo career and worked in collaboration with other musicians and writers. She has also written her own lyrics and music. Annlaug started her musical education in 1989 at the culture school in her home parish of Ulvik with Knut Hamre as her teacher. Annlaug received her higher education in music from Telemark College (as part of the Rauland Academy) and the Ole Bull Academy. There she was instructed by other teachers, including Leif Rygg, Vidar Lande, Håkon Høgemo, and Sigmund Eikås.

Annlaug recalls from her first session with Knut the tremulous sensation and the smell of crushed rosin as she took a fiddle out of its case for the very first time. Then they worked on learning fiddle tunes by ear. Just how it has always been done. Once their playing session was finished, Knut recorded a cassette of what they had learned so that she could listen to it at home. Knut was never tempted to make it more "exciting" by "gift-wrapping" his lessons at all. The subject was fiddle tunes, and they were more than enough. As she matured, they had plenty of discussions about dynamics and musical expression. Only the smallest part of their teaching revolved around technique, bowing styles, double stops, and so on.

"It baffles me how Knut has managed to sneak a good craft into the education of all of his students, without boringly cramming it in so that it felt like hard work."

Knut only ever interrupted Annlaug when she did something well, never to reprimand her or correct her mistakes. He is always lost in the music and serving his student. Nothing about Knut is shallow, and Annlaug doesn't feel like she has ever found the same amount of artistic freedom in other musicians and teachers as she has found in Knut. But she does wish that they had worked more on techniques and music theory, for example, and that he had been more structured and picky now and then.

"Everything was so open. His opinions would change from session to session, and it sometimes felt like there wasn't quite enough guidance. Knut didn't want to give a straight answer. Not then and still not now. At the same time, it didn't feel like I missed out on anything. I have found out many of these things by myself afterward anyway, or through other teachers. Maybe it would have been the wrong time to guide me too much, and this might have been exactly what Knut was thinking."

Later, once Annlaug had experienced different pedagogical approaches with slightly more set rules and guidance, she realized that this might not necessarily have been the best system, either. That was when she first truly realized the framework of Knut's method: Why he did what he did and why it worked so well.

"One of the best things about Knut as a teacher was the encouragement he gave. He encourages us all the time to seek out other teachers, and I have had many great ones. But even though I have spent years without any direct instruction from him and only met him sporadically, my own 'Hardanger fiddle master' is without a doubt Knut Hamre. Even now my sessions with Knut usually contain more discussions than fiddle playing. This master-student relationship will probably last forever."

Annlaug feels that things have gone full circle now, and feels a fresh desire to go back to learning Hardanger fiddle tunes. Which why she has sought out Knut's tutelage once more. She claims to have alternated between seeing the Hardanger tradition as oppressive and comforting. But she feels that Knut has always accepted this and encouraged her to do what she feels is right.

"Just look at how differently each of his students has turned out! I have often sensed an aura of honor and duty about people from Hardanger, a duty to be able to play and enjoy everything that comes from there. One especially feels this pressure at the various music colleges. But Hardanger fiddle music isn't the only type of music that has appealed to me, so soon I started seeking out different Norwegian traditions, together with folk music from other countries and other genres besides. The focus I have placed on pure Hardanger fiddle music has gone around in circles."

Still, Hardanger *slåttemusikk* has provided a solid foundation for Annlaug, like a safe upbringing. The most important thing she learned from Knut was a great love for music, and a strong urge to play so that music's true virtues take center stage, and in a style that revolves around playing and creating the best music possible, without care for written or unwritten rules.

"I think that is a possible reason why his pedagogical technique works so well. He teaches a completely unhindered style of playing, free of pretense and vanity."

Today, as a teacher of the Hardanger fiddle, Annlaug tries to do exactly what she thought was good about her tuition under Knut: to impart a passion for playing and a sense of freedom. But she also focuses more on technique and is rather picky, but tries to develop each student's personal style.

"When you substitute for another teacher, as I have often done in recent years, you need to allow yourself room to do things slightly differently. But now I no longer feel quite so self-assured when I come in through the door to my classrooms, for these students are never as happy to see me as they are to see Knut. I know that from personal experience."

TURID SPILDO

Born in 1967 and hailing from Granvin, Turid started her education at home with her grandfather, Einar Spildo. Later, she started receiving occasional lessons through the Hardanger Folk Music Association (Hardanger Spelemannslag) from fiddlers like Anders Kjerland, Olav Kvammen, Ingeleiv Kjerland Kvammen, Kristoffer Kjerland, and Håvard Kvandal.

She first received tuition from Knut Hamre when she was an adult, and had already received her musical education from Telemark College (as part of the Rauland Academy). Turid has also put out several CDs, both solo and together with Knut Hamre and the group Dvergmål. She is currently director at the Nerdrum Academy, a kind of Renaissance art school that focuses on painting. She is also a freelance musician of the Hardanger fiddle and *kveding*, or traditional Norwegian folk singing.

Turid's grandfather, Einar Spildo, would often stand waving at her when she came home from the school bus to ask her: "Are we playing today, then?" They lived on the same farm, so Turid can remember playing ever since she was a little girl. Einar was no pedagogical expert, but he did love to teach people, and was extremely patient. He had also memorized a vast repertoire of Hardanger tunes. Turid and her grandfather practiced around two or three times a week. Mostly he just sat there with his eyes closed and played systematically through each piece, without dividing them up in the slightest. In other words, you just had to keep up with him as best as you could manage. In the years between her 16th and 20th birthdays she lost her enthusiasm for fiddle playing until she had her desire rekindled by starting at the Rauland Academy, and even more so when she came home to Granvin and began studying under Knut Hamre. She had actually heard Knut playing and even met him when she was little, since he would often visit her grandfather or lead fiddle sessions for the Hardanger Fiddlers' Association. She only really began receiving regular sessions with Knut when she was in her early twenties, but these sessions lasted for years.

"Knut was a brilliant teacher who had a totally different way of listening than what I was used to. He is good at encouraging people and building up their self-esteem. He always takes you seriously, gauges your temperament and runs with it. I have learned a lot about my craft and various styles of fiddle tunes from Knut, but I have also learned a lot about different aspects of human life and various types of people. In their own way, both Knut and my grandfather were my most important teachers, but it was still crucial and right that Knut entered my life when he did."

Knut started up Turid's fire again. She sees it as a good thing she was grown up when she started learning from him. By then she was wiser and able to ask for exactly what she needed or was looking for. Another advantage was that she already knew her music, as well as a lot of Hardanger fiddle music from other parts of the country, which meant she didn't have to start from scratch. For this reason, Knut and Turid mostly worked on her repertoire and technique, as well as the keener details of the music, such as ornaments, tonality, and double stops. She also learned from Knut many big and challenging fiddle tunes that helped her improve her technique.

"Unfortunately, when you're still young and wet behind the ears, you pick up both good and the bad habits from your lessons. For example, I had brought my grandfather's stiff way of bowing along to Knut's sessions, and so Knut spent a lot of time helping me to iron out my bad habits."

The earnestness and lyricism surrounding Knut suited Turid well. They always had great chemistry, and they bounced off each other in conversation. Through the 1990s, Turid slowly entered the role of peer to Knut, which felt like a natural process. Although the *kappleikar* she was dragged to weren't quite her thing, she had positive and informative experiences at the concerts they performed together, along with every other form of collaboration they had.

"As a student, it makes you feel fantastic when your master asks you to collaborate with him on a project. I feel a little special whenever I get to be with Knut, and I can imagine the same goes for anyone else who plays with him. I have never been so calm as when I perform concerts alongside him. He has this aura that cancels out any anxiety. It never feels like a competition when you're around him. I don't think it's in his nature. Knut is also a prime mover who inspires people and ideas. I feel that I learned something about that, too: about putting things in motion and making things happen in my own life. He is incredibly innovative and somewhat reminds me of my husband, Odd Nerdrum."

Turid has her own students in both *kveding* and the Hardanger fiddle, but only teaches them occasionally. Some have only had a handful of lessons, and some have been tutored by her for a few years and more. She has also worked for a couple of years in the local culture school.

"I will gladly teach anyone who is really interested, but struggling with all the uninterested people you encounter at the culture school is much worse."

Turid believes that in terms of discipline, it is good for masters to teach students and maintain contact with the younger generation so that they develop themselves. She sees her own master-student education as the most optimal, starting with her grandfather at home and then later with Knut.

"A lot of good things have come from culture schools and music colleges. It is far better having these institutions than to have nothing at all. But I believe the framework of culture schools serves the students more than the teachers. My impression is that it can be immensely exhausting for the teachers. This factory-style production line of young students works best when they are tiny tots. But after that, the master-student style should prevail."

FRANK HENRIK ROLLAND

From Ulvik, born in 1973. In 1984, he started his education
through the Society of Free Schools (Folkeuniversitetet) in Ulvik
with Knut Hamre, and later studied at the culture school and
at the high school in Fagernes, where he specialized in folk
music. After that, he began taking private lessons. Frank Henrik
Rolland is A-Class fiddler and has released several CDs, both
alone and in collaboration with Knut Hamre and Åse Teigland.
From 1996 to the present day, he has been employed as the
County Musician in Hordaland, alongside teaching and holding
concerts, in addition to his archival work at the Hardanger Folk
Museum.

What Frank liked most about Knut was his one-on-one
approach. It allowed him to teach a completely different kind
of fiddle tunes, and it meant that Knut was in his element as a
teacher.

"Knut is no orchestra conductor, to put it simply. Maybe that's
why the classes of group tuition he led when I was young weren't
always successful. The folks there were always at different ages
and stages of playing. So it was probably a big challenge for
everyone."

The sessions with Knut mostly revolved around learning fiddle
tunes. There was never much talk about technique, yet Frank
slowly developed a better grasp of his craft through attempting
more and more technically demanding pieces of music.

But what stood out most of all in Knut's sessions were their
discussions. It's still like that today. Frank started asking
questions early on. Knut and Frank would discuss the expression

of each tune, the tune's history, and so on, but also day-to-day topics. Nothing is, or ever was, clear-cut with Knut.

"He never made so many comments that it felt negative, but would respect me making variations in the music. Within a certain aesthetic framework, he was open to anything that came to mind. It gave me the best feeling on earth to play with Knut when I was young. There was complete trust and chemistry from day one."

Frank believes his teacher was at the peak of his fiddling career when Frank started being tutored by him, and he has a variety of fond memories, including Knut playing so well at a *kappleik* that the crowd was left shrieking in ecstasy afterward. Frank feels lucky to have been taught by Knut during this period. Knut's pedagogical methods remind Frank somewhat of those used in the anthroposophical Rudolf Steiner schools.

"I mean, the way he inspired a joy for playing without nitpicking? The results of many wonderful and different fiddle players that have come from Knut indicate that his method has worked fantastically well."

Yet Frank understands that Knut's method isn't for everyone. He suspects that, although it might work if Knut's students are free and open-minded, it is probably very challenging if they are not. Some people require straightforward answers and a clear learning plan every now and then, while others are able to hear the connections and understand the structure of the music immediately.

"I do feel that Knut is more clear and to the point than he used to be in the 1980s, when he was more ambiguous. I think deciding which pedagogical methods work best is extremely dependent on the period, and the maturity of the student. For example, I remember that the substitute teachers we sometimes had when Knut was away all seemed rather strict and boring. In fact, I didn't really play any of the fiddle pieces I learned from them until I was older. I think I suppressed those teachers in a way. But today they are good friends, and I will happily learn fiddle tunes from the same people who used to be substitute teachers."

Frank suggests that Knut's most outstanding feature as a teacher is his sixth sense of his students' psychology. He *sees* everyone in this remarkable way, whether they are fantastic or less so.

"There is something about the way his personality and music fit together. Both sides of him shined out."

But if there is no chemistry between him and a student and Knut feels like he has nothing to offer, he can distance himself and not say a word. Another good thing about Knut's teaching style was when he brought his students along to visit other fiddle players. Frank was allowed to travel alongside Knut to see fiddlers like Anders Kjerland, Sigbjørn Bernhoft Osa, and Håvard Kvandal. He learned a lot from the latter. Knut would also bring students along to *kappleikar* or host them in his own home.

"Åse Teigland and I spent so much time together in Knut's home when we were younger that it almost made us wonder if we were part of the family. No other teachers from the culture school do things like that."

As Frank sees it, a master-student relationship with Knut will last a lifetime. It is a never-ending process. But nowadays, Frank loves to ask even more questions. He believes that Knut has become even wiser, too, perhaps due to his age, as well as his experiences and the lessons he has learned over a long life and career.

"In fact, he has generally become a lot more open with his words. Before, he would say almost nothing. His playing has also become a lot more level-headed than it was in the 1980s. He is pickier now and has less self-loathing too. That is a good thing."

When he was younger, Frank would copy as much as he could of Knut's playing. Today he spends more time listening to Knut's own muses, such as Anders Kjerland. Knut has always encouraged his students to take up different ways of doing something, then to fit them all together to form an original style.

"Knut himself does the same, and sometimes learns things from his own students. It seems he will never stop being curious, and he has a true love of music and of practicing and learning new things. He is just as hungry now as when he was fourteen years old. I try to do the same, but I'm hopeless compared to him!"

Frank sees Hardanger's master-student tradition as a good thing. But it is important to not just have one master. Neither should a master act like an answer sheet, but more like a guide. When Frank himself teaches students, he focuses on getting his students to master their craft while learning the Hardanger fiddle tunes and playing styles inside and out.

"If you want to play fiddle tunes well, it's important to have a firm foundation in your tradition. You need to find the essence and core of your music, or it will get watered down. I also think it's important for students to focus on learning the Hardanger repertoire if that is where they come from. This is helping the students cultivate their own sense of identity. After everything I have been taught, I feel obliged to give something back."

ÅSE TEIGLAND

From Utne, born in 1975. Åse freelances as a solo artist on the Hardanger Fiddle as well as in collaboration with a great many other musicians. She has been a particularly active *kappleik* competitor, taking part in concerts and CD recordings ever since she was a little girl. She has received a wealth of prizes and recognitions, including the A-Class category at the 2005 National *Kappleik*, becoming the second woman in Norwegian folk music history to do so. She enrolled at her culture school in 1985 when she was 9 years old, and Knut Hamre has been her main teacher ever since. She went on to receive teaching qualifications on top of her higher education at Telemark College (as part of the Rauland Academy) and the Ole Bull Academy. She is currently studying medicine.

Åse recalls how Knut never once told her she "had" to do anything. Now she is amazed by how he always managed to be so positive. Whenever she played a tune for him in one of these sessions, he would spontaneously come out with noises of approval, like "Mm!" or "Oh, yes!" She could tell they came right from the heart. Knut gave Åse the initiative early on by supplying her with the challenges she needed to learn instead of just telling her exactly what she was supposed to do. He would also bring her along to concerts and by the time she started middle school, he had already started using her as a substitute teacher for his younger students.

"With Knut, you learn things from the inside out, from within yourself and through your own experiences. You need to throw yourself into it. You might sometimes wonder how justified this teaching is, but you mature from these kind of challenges."

When she was growing up, Knut might ring up Åse out of the blue to say: "We have to go see Eivind Mo! Should we go tomorrow?" He would also take her along whenever Bjarne Herrefoss was in nearby Utne, and once they even went to visit him out in Skafså.

"I remember Bjarne pacing around the floor. I was eighteen, and back then I was a little star-struck being in the presence of such well-known figures as Bjarne. But I'm so glad that I was able to experience him, not to mention all the other people Knut has taken me to meet, since personally I'm not great at just popping in on people."

At the Rauland Academy she was taught by Stein Versto, but when she started at the Ole Bull Academy, Knut suggested that she take Ingeleiv Kjerland Kvammen and her husband, Olav Kvammen, as her teachers. Ingeleiv was a bit more strict in her feedback than Knut, and this was exactly what Åse wanted when she was studying there.

"I used to be more vulnerable to criticism when I was really young, but I needed more of it as I grew older. As teachers, the Kvammens were the complete opposite of Knut, and both were greatly important to me. I am immensely grateful to have been able to study at both schools."

Knut is quite dreamy and sometimes hazy as a person, but he is much clearer in a teaching environment. After a while, Åse actually would have rather liked it if Knut was more precise, and if he said when he disagreed with her aesthetic decisions. Now, as an adult, she has made different decisions, and wonders what he would think about them. She doubts his moral code would allow him to say much about them.

"He rarely spoke much with me about matters of expression, which is strange given how much I know he is occupied by things like that."

When Åse was young, she would get a lot of criticism for actively competing in *kappleikar*. This criticism mostly came about because her playing sounded too much like Knut's. Looking back, she realizes that it probably would have been a lot easier back then for him to introduce his own aesthetics into her personal style of musical expression. Yet she also knows that if he had done so, then she probably wouldn't have had the same amount of joy for playing.

"This journey isn't an obvious, straight line, but more like a spiral. Knut probably tries to provide what each individual person needs. When I studied at the teaching college and took modules in pedagogy and teaching methods, I remember thinking several times what a talented pedagogue Knut was! He has a great deal of patience and always calls out the good things in people. It is fascinating how students of Knut from the same generation have chosen such divergent paths and styles. It's clear that in practice, Knut's idea of anyone and everyone being able to have their own identity has worked."

On the conflict between large educational institutions and the one-on-one master-student relationships, Åse would say "Yes, please!" to both. For her, the good thing about a standardized education is that you meet many other people, both students and teachers. But Åse also points out that there needs to be a lot of room set aside for individualism within all art schools, not just readymade learning plans and aesthetic ideals.

"Challenges in certain systems often arise when people start abusing their position and trying to steer their students in terms of what they should focus on, who they should learn from, and so on."

This is why Åse has much more faith in one-on-one teaching and close relationships, although it is better to have several close relationships with more than one master. Otherwise, she believes that in order to teach their students well, a master needs to be generous, inclusive, and willing to give something back.

"It's not about calling attention to yourself or pushing truths on other people, but about calling out the students' true selves. Anyone who does the former is no great master."

Nowadays when Åse is teaching her own students, she tries to imitate the best things she remembers about Knut's teaching style, and uses these points as a kind of curriculum. At the same time, however, she is pickier about the things she was missing when she was young. She finds it challenging when she doesn't agree with something her student does, but tries to think back to Knut and let them find it out for themselves. Åse also encourages them to listen to recordings so that they become aware of different ways of doing things, and let their style be colored by that.

There is no doubt that Knut is the teacher Åse learned most from. He will always be an important part of her life. She still calls him up to ask for advice, not just as a musician, but about any aspect of life. He is a great accompanist, in every sense of the word.

"Knut also rings me when he has thought and mulled over something, even though he always warns people never to overthink! We are from two different generations, but it never feels that way."

Cry not, little bugs!

Even stars must part,

From those they love.

Kobayashi Issa

2013 | After waking up early morning in Bergen, I have
now arrived at Ålvik for its international artist residency,
Kunstnarhuset Messen, which Knut occasionally rents for
practice. This enormous, hallowed red building used to be
the head office for the factory nearby. Nowadays it is used by
artists from the world over who might need a space to work in
for short (or longer) periods. Echoes of fiddling fill the corridor
as I make my way upstairs to the second floor, where Knut is
staying. Knut keeps playing as I open the door. In the practice
room there is a timeworn sofa, two chairs, and a small table on
which to lay a fiddle or two. The walls are covered by brown
wallpaper that looks ready to peel off at any moment from water
damage. Nothing else. I smile a little at the thought that Knut
isn't particularly materialistic. The old curtains, which have
probably hung there since the late 1970s, sway gently into the
room in time with the faint breeze from the fjord nearby. Today
I am going to learn a new fiddle tune. Maybe two, if the first one
isn't too long and we manage to squeeze them both in before the
afternoon, when Knut has to meet with a few students from the
culture school. It has been a while since we last saw each other.
Knut's playing stops as he looks up at me and smiles.

"Last night I dreamt about Bjarne Herrefoss."

"Oh? What happened in the dream?"

"I dreamt I was sitting in a huge, green pasture, completely alone, and then this big stout man came walking toward me across the field with an unusual gait and a fiddle case in one hand. It was Bjarne. I was a grown man in the dream, like I am now, but I felt that same intense, burning desire to hear him play that I had when I was younger, listening to him on the radio or at *kappleikar*. I didn't say a word, but Bjarne stopped right in front of me, looked down, and calmly said, 'Hi.' He then kept walking across the green field. I stayed where I was and watched him slowly moving away, carrying his fiddle case in one hand."

"I can see that you still miss your dear friend and teacher."

"Yes, I do. Even though I have accepted that the wheel has to keep turning."

Tears begin to fill Knut's eyes more and more, until he shakes them off and pulls himself together.

"How about learning 'Vassendaslåtten' as played by Eirik Medås? I was thinking I might teach it to you today."

"Of course. I hope you live to be a really old man, Knut."

"I promise I will. As long as you promise to come tune my fiddle!"

KNUT HAMRE
TIMELINE

Born in Voss Hospital on the 3rd of March 1952.

His parents were Knut J. Hamre from Folkedal (1917-1992) and Marta Hamre from Voss (1917-1984).

In 1939, Knut and Marta settled on the Nylendo farmstead in Folkedal, Granvin.

Knut Hamre had a brother twelve years older than himself, Johannes Hamre (1940-2013), as well as a twin brother who passed away shortly after his birth in 1952.

Began actively participating in the Hardanger Fiddlers' Association in 1963 and continues to do so today.

Started receiving tuition from Anders Kjerland in 1964, in Granvin.

In 1967, Knut won his first *kappleik* in Sogndal, competing in the C-Class category for competitors younger than 18.

Between 1967 and 1970, Knut was a bricklaying apprentice in Voss. He worked as a bricklayer until 1981.

In 1972, he met Aud Laingen Hamre (b. 1947). They married in 1974 and settled in Folkedal, where they took over the farm then owned by Knut's parents.

Before long they had children: Ingebjørg in 1975, Anna in 1978, and Bjørnar in 1979. Today, Knut Hamre has four grandchildren.

In 1974, he became the youngest-ever winner of the A-Class category at the National *Kappleik* (Landskappleik) in Oppdal.

In 1980, Knut recorded his first LP in collaboration with Leif Rygg.

Between 1981 and 1984, he worked as a chimney sweep in Granvin.

Between 1982 and 1984, he contributed to free tuition in Ulvik on the Hardanger fiddle.

From 1985 to 1992, he worked at the Hardanger Music School.

From 1984 to 1993, he found work as an archivist at the Hardanger Folk Museum in Utne, teaching all the while.

From 1992 to 1994, he was employed as the County Musician in Hordaland.

From 1993 to 1996, he was awarded a three-year arts grant from the Norwegian state. He achieved many things during this period, including the recording of his solo album, *Fargespel*.

In 1994, he started teaching again at Hardanger's Culture School and was employed there continuously until the spring of 2014, when Knut retired. He still gives private lessons and teaches at Master Class Hardanger.

Knut released a number of CDs in this period, both solo and in collaboration with other students and peers, in addition to receiving prizes and grants. He held a great deal of concerts in Norway and abroad in countries such as Japan, the United States, Russia, and Germany.

DISCOGRAPHY

Nøringen (LP), Leif Rygg and Knut Hamre, Heilo/Grappa Musikkforlag, 1980

Slik spelar Knut (MC), solo, Spelarhaugen, 1984

Norwegian Folk Songs and Peasant Dances from Op. 66 and Op. 72, Geir Botnen, Reidun Horvei and Knut Hamre, Simax, 1993

Fargespel, solo, Heilo/Grappa Musikkforlag, 1994

Toneflaum, Hallvard T. Bjørgum, Bjarne Herrefoss and Knut Hamre, SYLVCD, 1998

Å, Knut Hamre, Steve Tibbetts, Marc Anderson and Turid Spildo, Hannibal Records, 1999

Håstabøslåttar, Knut Hamre, Åse Teigland and Frank Rolland, Heilo/ Grappa Musikkforlag, 1999

I Halldors ånd, Trio Hardanger, 2L, 2003

Rosa i botnen, Knut Hamre, Benedicte Maurseth, Nils Økland, Sigbjørn Apeland and Håkon *Stene*, Heilo/Grappa Musikkforlag, 2006

Ferd, solo, Heilo/Grappa Musikkforlag, 2010

Eg ser deg, Knut Hamre, Turid Spildo and Johannes Martens, Ta:lik, 2011

Anima, Knut Hamre, Benedicte Maurseth, Nils Økland, Philippe Pierlot and Elisabeth Seitz, Heilo/Grappa Musikkforlag, 2012

Spelarhola, Knut Hamre, Åse Teigland and Alexander Aga Røynstrand, Ta:lik, 2014

Slåttar frå Granvin, Knut Hamre, Heilo/Grappa Musikkforlag , 2018

PRIZES AND AWARDS

Kongepokal (An annual trophy awarded at *kappleikar*) 1981

Myllargutprisen (An annual prize awarded to folk musicians in honor of Torgeir Augundsson) 1986

Edvard Grieg-prisen (An annual prize awarded to musicians and composers for communicating the music of Edvard Grieg in a special way) 1993

Spelemannsprisen (An annual Norwegian Grammy awarded to musicians) for *Toneflaum*, 1998

Hilmar Alexandersens minnepris (A prize awarded in memory of Hilmar Alexandersen) 1993

Statens treårige arbeidsstipend (A three-year arts grant from the Norwegian state) 1993-1996

Heidersmedlem i Landslaget for Spelemenn (Honorary Fellow of the National Association of Folk Music, today called Folk Org) 2004

Anders Kjerlands minnepris (A prize awarded in memory of Anders Kjerland) 2000

Kommandør av Den kongelege Norske St. Olavs Orden (Commander of the Royal Norwegian Order of Saint Olav) 2017

NATIONAL KAPPLEIKAR

Wins in A-Class Category:

1974, Oppdal

1978, Fagernes

1981, Oslo

1984, Odda

1985, Otta

1987, Sogndal

2000, Voss

SUGGESTED LISTENING

Below you will find a brief overview of where to obtain recordings of the various musical pieces that are referred to in *To Be Nothing*:

KNUT HAMRE

See "Discography" for titles of releases by Knut Hamre.

You can get hold of these recordings in CD form, or download digital copies from various websites, such as the record company homepage, www.grappa.no, and their subsidiaries, Heilo and Simax Classics.

The album *Å* was released by the now-defunct record label Hannibal Records. You can still find it on www.stevetibbetts.com/a/ or Amazon.

Older releases on either cassette or vinyl, as well as various archived recordings of Knut Hamre, can be procured by contacting the Hardanger Folk Music Archives at the Hardanger Folk Museum in Utne. http://www.hardangerogvossmuseum.no

BJARNE HERREFOSS

Draumespel include some of the best moments of Bjarne Herrefoss "on record" and at *kappleikar* in the period between 1958 and 1981. CD copies of this collection aren't easy to get hold of anymore, but the album is distributed by fiddler Knut Buen's label, Buen Kulturverkstad. You can find digital copies of these releases on websites such as Amazon, iTunes, Phonophile, Spotify, Tidal, and more.

Toneflaum (SYLVCD, 1998) is a recording of solo fiddle tunes by Bjarne Herrefoss, Knut Hamre, and Hallvard T. Bjørgum. On the record, you can hear top-quality fiddling from each of the three traditional regions of the Hardanger fiddle: Telemark, Hardanger, and Setesdal. The recording won the Spelemannsprisen (Grammy Award for traditional music) in 1998. The physical CD is sold out, but is still available on iTunes and Amazon, as well as Spotify.

ANDERS KJERLAND

Helsing med tonefylgje. Anders Kjerland, hardingfele. A collection of private recordings of Anders Kjerland done by fiddle maker Håvard Kvandal in 1967. Released by Aksent in 2018. Available both digitally and on CD. Order at www.aksent.no

The Norwegian broadcasting corporation, NRK, made almost 500 recordings of Anders Kjerland between 1948 and 1979, and a selection from 1950-66 was released as the solo album *Hardingtonar* (LP and cassette, 1987). For a copy of these recordings, contact the Hardanger Folk Music Archives at the Hardanger Folk Museum in Utne. http://www.hardangerogvossmuseum.no

Four other fiddle tunes by Anders Kjerland can be found on the recording *Slåttar frå Voss, Hardanger og Krødsherad*, forming part of the serial album, *Norsk Folkemusikk*, which was rereleased on CD in 2009. Check out www.talik.no

GLOSSARY OF SELECTED TERMS

Bordunspel (double stop) – The technique in which two notes are bowed or plucked simultaneously on a stringed instrument. Although the word "stop" suggests that the notes should be played by pressing your fingers down and "stopping" the vibrations, you can also play open notes. In Hardanger fiddle music it is quite common to include open notes. Many refer to it as a *borduntone* (drone) when notes don't change yet harmonize constantly with the melody being played on the main strings. Therefore, many find it challenging to separate the main melody from the constant harmony in Hardanger fiddle music. Triple stops and quadruple stops refer to playing three and four notes at the same time, respectively. Together these are known as "multiple stops." When only one string is played at a time, it is referred to as *einstrengspel*.

Equal temperament was adopted in the 18th century and is still in use today. The octave is divided into twelve precisely equal semitones. According to acoustical theory, all of these are out of tune. The great advantage of equal temperament is that it makes all keys, and also modulations between them, equally available. In reality, no one is actually able to play or sing like this. Modern keyboard instruments are usually equal-tempered, though some electronic instruments can be instantly retuned to historical scales. By contrast, Hardanger fiddle strings are tuned and played in a variety of alternative temperaments. They provide many possible choices when it comes to pitch, since you can alter the size of each interval simply by changing where you place your fingers.

Fylkesmusikar (county musician) – A role awarded to musicians by various counties of Norway. Similar to a poet laureate, each Fylkesmusikar is expected to compose, teach, and perform music on behalf of their appointed county.

Hardingfele (Hardanger fiddle) – *Hardingfele* is the Norwegian term for the Hardanger fiddle. A person who comes from Hardanger is called a "Harding," and the Hardanger fiddle was originally built, shaped, and spread from Hardanger. Hence the term *Hardingfele*, "a fiddle from

Hardanger." Today the oldest Hardanger fiddle we know about is the famous "Jaastad fiddle," signed and dated in 1651 by Ole Jonsen Jaastad (1621-1694) from Ullensvang parish in Hardanger. Yet there is no doubt that, prior to Telemark's takeover in the 1800s, the craftsmen who had the largest impact on the development of the Hardanger fiddle were Isak Nielsen Skaar (1669-1759) and his son, Trond Isaksen Flatebø (1713-1772), both from Kvam parish. The Hardanger fiddle is especially characterized by its rich decorations, understrings (sympathetic strings), and its flat bridge. These characteristics make it easy to use a kind of polyphonic technique (*bordunspel*, or double stops). We don't know for sure the origin and the construction of the instrument. Research shows that there existed an older and smaller type of fiddle in the region before the violin was built. It's reasonable to assume that the early Hardanger fiddle construction is a mix of the older type that already existed and the violin.

Kappleik (plural: *kappleikar*) – A traditional folk music competition of Norway, dating back to the late 1800s. Today there are dozens of official *kappleikar* taking place in various counties of Norway, as well as one annual national competition called *Landskappleik*, which lasts for five days. The modern *Landskappleik* encompasses not only fiddle playing, but also many other folk instruments and art forms, such as traditional dancing and instrument making.

The Hardanger fiddle competition is usually split into four different categories: the D-Category is for fiddle players older than 60, the C-Category is for fiddlers aged between 12 and 18, the B-Category for those over 18, and the A-Category is reserved for the very best fiddle players who have received a certain high score twice in the B-Category.

Kveding – A traditional Norwegian style of folk singing, characterized by its equal temperament, rich embellishments, and often-flowing rhythm. The word derives from the Norse *kvad* or *kvede*, which means "to tell a poem rhythmically and in a sacred way." A *kvedar* often sings a capella and uses consonants in the language as important melodic elements. *Kveding* is much closer to natural speech than some other song traditions. Each *kvedar*'s voice is usually heavily affected by their own dialect.

Microtone is any interval distinctly smaller than a semitone (half-tone). This is highly present in Norwegian folk music as well as Arabic, Eastern European, and Indian music.

Mode is usually referring to one of the scales in the medieval system of ecclesiastical church modes. The term "modal" is commonly used to describe music which makes use of harmonies and/or melodies based on a mode rather than a major or minor scale. Modal music usually doesn't involve key changes within individual pieces.

Old-time dances (gamaldans/runddans) – An umbrella term for European dance forms that came to Norway from the end of the 18th century onward. Old-time dances are often associated with accordion- and diatonic button accordion-based music. Typical dance forms are the schottische, waltz, mazurka, and polka.

Ornaments/Embellishments – Notes that are extraneous to the main notes of a melodic line, serving to "grace" (decorate or embellish) it, and sometimes also serving to enhance the harmony or make the rhythm more incisive. In Norwegian they are called *triller*.

Scordatura (*felestille* in Norwegian) – A term applied largely to lutes, guitars, viols, and the violin family to designate a tuning other than the normal, established one. Scordatura was first introduced early in the 16th century and enjoyed a particular vogue between 1600 and 1750. It offered novel colors, timbres and sonorities, alternative harmonic possibilities, and, in some cases, extension of an instrument's range. It could also assist in imitating other instruments, and facilitate the execution of various passages involving wide intervals, intricate string crossing, or unconventional double stopping. North American and Scottish fiddlers commonly adopt "open" tunings, which emphasize particular keys, for greater resonance when playing chords and arpeggios and to facilitate the use, as drones, of open strings adjacent to the one on which the melody is being played. The term scordatura has also been applied to instruments which have no standard tuning, such as the viola d'amore, the lyra viol, and various folk instruments including the Norwegian Hardanger fiddle.

Slått (tune) – From this word we derive the term *slåttemusikk*. It is the everyday term for a piece of Norwegian instrumental folk music. The word *slått* derives from the verb *å slå*, or "to hit." This suggests that *slåttemusikk* was originally played by hitting or plucking the strings with one's fingers, just like a harp or *langeleik* (a kind of Norwegian dulcimer). *Slåttemusikk* therefore probably existed before the Hardanger fiddle did, and the fiddle bow must have arrived later into Norwegian folk music than this term. The term used for a piece of *slåttemusikk* varies from place to place in Norway. The term *slått* is traditionally used in Telemark and the central parts of Vestlandet and Numedal. Fiddlers in Hallingdal and Valdres use the word *lått* (from the verb *å låte*, or "to sound"). Setesdal uses the term *slag* (probably of roughly the same origins as *slått*), while Gudbrandsdalen refers to each fiddle tune as *leik* or *læk* ("play"). *Slått* is also an umbrella term for different types of *slåttemusikk*, such as *springar, gangar, halling, lydarslått, brureslått, bruremarsj,* and *huldreslått*.

Triplets – A term used to describe the dividing of a single beat into three.

Understrings, sympathetic strings, or *resonance strings* are thin steel strings which lie under the playing strings. These strings aren't unique to the Hardanger fiddle. You find them in many other types of instruments, such as the sitar, sarangi, hurdy-gurdy, viola d'amore, and Swedish nyckelharpa. Precise tuning is essential so that when the playing strings are bowed, the understrings vibrate in sympathy.

Modern-day Hardanger fiddles tend to have either four or five understrings, but this has changed over time. The renowned "Jaastad fiddle" from 1651, for example, has only two understrings.

SECONDARY LITERATURE

Aksdal, Bjørn. *Felemakertradisjonen i Hardanger,* article from the text enclosed within the CD *Rosa i botnen,* Heilo/Grappa Musikkforlag, 2006.

Aksdal, Bjørn. *Felemakarane i Botnen – hardingar og europearar,* article from the text enclosed within the CD *Anima,* Heilo/Grappa Musikkforlag, 2012.

Aksdal, Bjørn. *Hardingfela, felemakerne og instrumentets utvikling,* Tapir Akademisk Forlag, Trondheim, 2009.

Aksdal, Bjørn, et al. *Fanitullen. Innføring i norsk og samisk folkemusikk,* Universitetsforlaget, Oslo, 1993.

Allkunne. http://www.allkunne.no.

Berge, Rikard. *Myllarguten – Gibøen,* Aschehougs forlag, Oslo 1908 and Noregs Boklag, Oslo, 1972.

Espeland, Åsmund. *Me tar det på gamlemåten. Hovudfagsoppgåve i etnomusikologi,* Griegakademiet at the University of Bergen, 2003.

Fosse, Jon. *Andvake,* Det Norske Samlaget, Oslo, 2007.

Fosse, Jon. *Dikt, 1986–2000,* Det Norske Samlaget, Oslo, 2001.

Fosse, Jon. *Poems,* Shift Fox Press, Canada, 2014. Translated by May-Brit Akerholt.

Fosse, Jon. *Wakefulness,* Dalkey Press, London, 2016. Translated by May-Brit Akerholt.

Hauge, Olav H. *Dikt i samling,* Det Norske Samlaget, Oslo, 2000.

Hauge, Olav H. *Lagnaden gjer mange til heltar. Aforismar i utval,* Det Norske Samlaget, Oslo, 2001.

Hauge, Olav H. *Luminous Places,* White Pine Press, New York, 2016. Translated by Olav Grinde.

Haukanæs, Th.S. (Thrond Sjursen). *Granvins Saga, første del,* A. Garnæs Boktrykkeri, Bergen, 1904.

Haukanæs, Th.S. *Granvins Saga, anden og tredje del,* N. Nilssen og Søns boktrykkeri, Bergen, 1915.

Hofmo, Gunvor. *Samlede dikt*, Gyldendal Norsk Forlag, Oslo, 2010.

Hopkins, Pandora. *Aural Thinking in Norway: Performance and Communication with the Hardangerfele*, Human Sciences Press, 1986.

Hus, Oddmund, et al. *Hardanger Spelemannslag 50 år*, Hardanger Spelemannslag, 1998.

Kvifte, Tellef. *On variability in the performance of hardingfele tunes— and paradigms in ethnomusicological research*, Taragot Sounds, 2017.

Maurseth, Benedicte. *Læremeisterens læremeistrar*, article in national Norwegian paper, Dag og Tid, #24, 18 June 2010.

Maurseth, Benedicte. *Kjære lydarar*, essay included in the attached text of the CD Alde, Heilo/Grappa Musikkforlag, Oslo, 2010.

Merton, Thomas. *The Way of Chuang Tzu*, New Directions Book, New York, 1997.

Ofsdal, Steinar. *Tonaliteten i folkemusikken*, article in Norsk Folkemusikklag's magazine, Oslo, 2006.

Olafsen, Olaf. *Granvin i fortid og nutid, en bygdebok*, Skaars Boktrykkeri, 1922.

Riise, Hildegun. *Plukke stjerner med hendene*. *Dikt utvalde av Hildegun Riise*, Det Norske Samlaget, Oslo, 1997.

Ruud, Even. *Musikk som kommunikasjon og samhandling*. *Teoretiske perspektiv på musikkterapien*, Solum Forlag, Oslo, 1990.

Store Norske Leksikon. http://www.snl.no

Stubseid, Gunnar. *Frå spelemannslære til akademi*. *Om folkemusikkopplæring i Noreg, med hovudvekt på slåttemusikken på hardingfele*, Forlaget Folkekultur, Bergen, 1992.

Suzuki, Shunryū. *Zen-sinn, begynner sinn, revidert utgåve*, Buddhistforbundets forlag, Oslo, 2000.

Ta:lik, http://www.talik.no

INTERVIEWS AND CONVERSATIONS

Bjørn Aksdal

Hallvard T. Bjørgum

Annlaug Børsheim

Jon Fosse

Odd Nerdrum

Steinar Ofsdal

Frank Rolland

Turid Spildo

Lajla Renate Buer Storli

Åse Teigland

Steve Tibbetts

Stig Valberg

IMAGE CREDITS

Knut Bry. Photo of the "Jaastad-fiddle." The oldest existing Hardanger fiddle, made in 1651 by Ole Jonsen Jaastad (1621-1694) from Lofthus, Hardanger (Cover Photo)

Vidar Herre / Hordaland Newspaper (Avisa Hordaland) (Frontispiece)

Knut Bry. Detail of "Jaastad-fiddle" (p. 0)

Unknown photographer. Photo of Eide, center of Granvin, taken around 1890s (p. 8)

Giovanni Trimboli. Knut Hamre playing at a midsummer wedding in 1963. Photo was once used as a postcard (p. 12-13)

Samuel J. Beckett. Photo of Eidfjord municipality, taken around 1915 (p. 16)

Unknown photographer. Photo of Eide, center in Granvin, and the Granvin fjord taken in 1890 (p. 18)

Knut Bry. Front fiddle is the "Jaastad-fiddle." Second fiddle was made by Isak Nielsen Skaar (1669-1759), and third fiddle, "Lofthus-fiddle," was made by his son Trond Isaksen Flatebø (1713-1772). Both makers came from Kvam, Hardanger (p. 24-25)

Axel Lindahl. Courtesy of Sverre Lillegraven (p. 38-39)

Courtesy of Sigrid Røynstrand (p. 40)

Courtesy of Knut Hamre (p. 41)

Courtesy of Kjell Herheim (p. 42)

Photo taken by Ingerid Jordal. Courtesy of Hardanger Folk Museum (Hardanger Folkemuseum) (p. 44)

Unknown photographer. View of Skjervet, Granvin, Hardanger (p. 46-47)

Unknown photographer. Archives from the fiddling magazine *Spelemannsbladet* (p. 48)

Courtesy of Knut A. Kjerland (pp. 54-55, 58-59, 110)

Sigmund Krøvel-Velle / Hallingdølen Newspaper (p. 70)

Bernt Balchen. Courtesy of Martha Balchen (p. 78-79)

Odd E. Nerbø / Archives at the Olav H. Hauge Centre (pp. 86, 232-233)

Bodil Cappelen (p. 92-93)

Unknown photographer. Skjervefossen, waterfall in Granvin, Hardanger (p. 100)

Photo taken by Arne Sigurd Haugen / Archives from the fiddling magazine *Spelemannsbladet* (p. 103)

Hulda Berntzens publishing (p. 107)

Kjell Bitustøyl. Photo of Knut Hamre and his student Alexander A. Røynstrand (1990-) at a Landskappleik in Våga in 2002 (p. 114)

Unknown photographer. Photo of Granvin church built in 1726 (p. 140)

Knut Bry. Detail of the "Lofthus-fiddle" (p. 150)

Kjell Herheim. Photo of Knut Hamre playing at a National *kappleik* in Voss, 2000. Knut won that day (p. 160)

Brynhildsen. Courtesy of Knut A. Kjerland. Photo of fiddle player Nils Eide "Tråen" (1873-1946) from Granvin (p. 168)

Courtesy of Kjellaug Velken (p. 172-173)

Courtesy of Steve Tibbetts (p. 181)

Unknown photographer. Photo of fiddle player Halldor Meland (1884-1976) from Ullensvang, Hardanger (p. 182)

Knut Bry (pp. 188, 224)

Jan M. Lillebø / National paper Bergens Tidende. Photo of Knut Hamre and Benedicte Maurseth at a fiddle lesson, taken in 1993 (p. 202-203)

Unknown photographer. Photo of women and children from the Seim farm in Upper Granvin, Hardanger (p. 220)

Kjell Bitustøyl. Photo of Knut Hamre taken in Shetland (p. 246)

ACKNOWLEDGMENTS

The author would especially like to thank: David Rothenberg for being committed to putting this book out in English, Bruce Thomson for his translation, Tyran Grillo and Clare Salaman for additional help with the manuscript; Steve Tibbetts, Knut Utler, Harald Knutsen, Kjell Bitustøyl, Sverre Lillegraven, and Knut A. Kjerland for help finding photos for the book. Also Knut Bry, Jan M. Lillebø, Odd E. Nerbø, Vidar Herre, Sigmund Krøvel-Velle, Kjell Herheim, Ingerid Jordal, and other private owners of photos for giving us permission to print them. The author and publisher would like to thank in addition NORLA, Ole Melkeråen, Statens Kunstnerstipend (National Arts Grant), and the Hardanger Folk Music Association (Hardanger Spelemannslag) for financial support of this English translation.

www.maurseth.net

ENDNOTES

[1] A microtone is any interval distinctly smaller than a semitone (half-tone). This is highly present in Norwegian folk music as well as Arabic, Eastern European, and Indian music.

[2] "Mode" usually refers to one of the scales in the medieval system of church modes (or ecclesiastical modes). The term "modal" is commonly used to describe music which makes use of harmonies and/or melodies based on a mode rather than a major or minor scale.

[3] The nickname means "Millerboy." Augundsson was an exceptional fiddle player from Telemark. He enjoyed wealth and fame in Norway during his lifetime, which was unusal at the time, and is today considered the best-known Hardanger fiddler of all time.

[4] *Dåm* is a Norwegian word connoting a spiritual and soulful feeling in the music that is ultimately indefinable and impossible to explain in technical terms. Still, it is something one can feel as a listener. In the context of Norwegian folk music it is often used as a word of honor and admiration. When music is technically weak yet nonetheless "ingenious," *dåm* is used for lack of other technical words to describe the atmosphere in and around the music. *Dåm* is not something one can learn or train for, but something one has as a player or not. It may be what flamenco players call "duende."

[5] Equal temperament means that each of the intervals between each of the twelve semitones in an octave is the same. The norm in Norwegian folk music is to also play microtones between these equal semitones.

[6] *Bunad* is an umbrella term for traditional Norwegian costumes. They exist in many different variations around the country. In the broadest sense, *bunad* encompass a range of both traditional rural clothes mostly dating to the 18th and 19th centuries as well as 20th-century folk costumes. In its narrow sense, the word *bunad* refers only to clothes designed in the early 20th century that are loosely based on traditional costumes. The word *bunad* is itself a 20th-century invention.

[7] *Folkemusikkhalvtimen* is a radio program about folk music that has been broadcast every Sunday on NRK since 1931. For folk music lovers this half hour, now a whole hour, has long been considered a sacred time of the week, but has also been a highly controversial program for those who don't like Norwegian folk music.

[8] *Huldreslått* is a special genre in the Hardanger fiddle repertoire often connected with a *hulder,* a female forest creature. The name *hulder* derives from a root meaning "covered" or "secret." We don't know much about the purpose of this genre, when or how it was used, but it seems there existed a larger repertoire in this style earlier that is forgotten today. A *Huldreslått* can have a steady pulse, but the atmosphere in these tunes tells us they must have been played for other special rituals or ceremonies rather than for dances. They are always played in unusual fiddle tunings, and are connected with stories of a fiddle player who falls a sleep. He dreams of a *hulder* who sings a tune to him, and when he wakes up, he plays the tune given to him in his dream.

[9] *Bokmål* and *Nynorsk* are two different written languages in Norway. *Bokmål* is the majority language, much influnced by the Danish language, since Norway was ruled under Denmark for several hundred years. *Nynorsk* is a written language formed during the 1800s based on different Norwegian dialects. There is a constant battle between those who are against and those who are pro *Nynorsk* and *Bokmål* in Norway. Olav H. Hauge wrote only in *Nynorsk.* The book you are now reading was originally written in *Nynorsk.*

[10] The idea of *kulturskule* came from the politics of the socialists and social democrats, who in the 1960s pushed for art and music to be accessible for everyone, whether one lived in a city or a more remote area, whether one was rich or poor. Anyone could apply to music schools and the costs for families were low since it was, and still is, largely subsidized by taxes. In the districts, teachers commonly travel to where students live.